MAKING SENSE OF
SPIRITUAL
WARFARE

Books by
Eddie Smith
FROM BETHANY HOUSE PUBLISHERS

Breaking the Enemy's Grip

How to Be Heard in Heaven

*Strategic Prayer**

Making Sense of Spiritual Warfare

*with Michael Hennen

MAKING SENSE OF
SPIRITUAL
WARFARE

EDDIE SMITH

BETHANYHOUSE
Minneapolis, Minnesota

Published by Bethany House Publishers
11400 Hampshire Avenue South
Bloomington, Minnesota 55438

Bethany House Publishers is a division of
Baker Publishing Group, Grand Rapids, Michigan.

Printed in the United States of America

In keeping with biblical principles of creation stewardship, Baker Publishing Group advocates the responsible use of our natural resources. As a member of the Green Press Initiative, our company uses recycled paper when possible. The text paper of this book is comprised of 30% post-consumer waste.

green press INITIATIVE

Library of Congress Cataloging-in-Publication Data

Smith, Eddie.
    Making sense of spiritual warfare : finding clarity about the combatants, weapons, precautions, goals, victory / Eddie Smith.
        p. cm.
    Summary: "A clear explanation of what spiritual warfare is, what the Bible says about it, who is involved, what the outcome will be, and what part people today play in the age-old conflict"—Provided by publisher.
    ISBN 978-0-7642-0393-0 (pbk. : alk. paper) 1. Spiritual warfare. I. Title.

BV4509.5.S62177   2008
235'.4—dc22

2008014289

I dedicate this book to Alice,
my wife and partner in ministry.
Alice is the wisest and most balanced
spiritual warrior I know.

ABOUT THE AUTHOR

EDDIE SMITH is the co-founder and president of the U.S. Prayer Center, a cross-denominational prayer leader and teacher, and an internationally known conference speaker. He is also a bestselling author of several books, including, with his wife, Alice, *Spiritual Housecleaning*. Before founding the U.S. Prayer Center in 1990, Eddie and Alice served sixteen years in itinerant evangelism and fourteen years in local churches. The Smiths make their home in Houston, Texas.

CONTENTS

INTRODUCTION

Search the Internet for anything "spiritual" and you'll discover more than a hundred *million* entries. Few topics engender more passion and more wild behavior than *spiritual warfare*. But what exactly is spiritual warfare? Can anyone explain it in layman's terms? Is every Christian to be involved in it?

What's the point of spiritual warfare? How should we view the bizarre actions and outlandish claims of some who seem to assume that Satan is omnipresent and omniscient to the point that he spends his days looking for ways to interact with them and destroy their lives?

Making Sense of Spiritual Warfare is intended as a pastoral book, written to bring balance and wisdom to the arena. It will begin with the basics and will challenge the conclusions of both those who deny the existence of the battle and also those who've determined that it should be everyone's highest priority.

The purposes of spiritual warfare vary from casting out a demon to warring against principalities, from seeing solutions to personal or family problems to seeing the salvation of the nations. I don't claim to have all the answers. But I do have more questions than most. And questions are good. They press us into thinking. They challenge us to seek God and to study His Word.

My prayer is that here you'll find answers to some of your lingering questions. Even if I do little more than challenge your ideas, *Making Sense of Spiritual Warfare* will be time well spent, for each of us must be prepared to give reasons for why we believe as we do.

If you're new to all of this, relax, enjoy, and seek to learn. There are no "specialists." Let the Spirit teach you. Take what I've written here to the Word of God and to the Holy Spirit. He has promised to guide you into all truth.

CHAPTER 1

THE GREATEST WAR

There's a preteen rite of passage in the South, one that's especially fun (and funny) for the older kids. They get to initiate unsuspecting younger kids by taking them "snipe hunting."

It was my turn to prove myself. The following week I would turn nine—just in time to demonstrate my manly hunting-and-gathering skills on what I'd later discover was an imaginary creature.

Okay, I thought to myself, *I'm sitting here in the forest alone, under this oak tree. I wonder how long I'll have to wait. It's almost midnight.* How *did the guys tell me to hold my pillowcase?*

(Time passes.)

What was that? Am I hearing things? It's scary out here in the dark. I wonder how the guys are doing. It's getting harder and harder to hold open this pillowcase . . . but I gotta catch the snipe when it's chased my way. Gotta *stay awake . . .* gotta *stay awake. . . .*

You've probably guessed that my trickster friends never located a snipe or even bothered looking for one. Remember? *Snipes are imaginary!* (as catchable little forest creatures with exaggerated, fictional characteristics, anyway). So of course I didn't get to catch one. The big kids had merely returned to the comfort of the camp while trying to stifle their laughter. They enjoyed a good night's sleep while I sat in the woods until I couldn't keep my eyes open. I awoke the next morning, under that big oak, empty pillowcase in my lap.

I was furious when I discovered the deception and realized I was the brunt of their jokes. I wasn't furious the next year, though, when *I* was old enough to take a "new boy" snipe hunting.

* * *

Invisible isn't the same as *imaginary.* Spiritual warfare—unseen spiritual combat that's largely intangible and immaterial—is difficult to define, but it *is* real. Even so, some ask, "If it's invisible, how can we know it actually exists?"

First, we know spiritual warfare exists because *God demonstrates its principles* in His Word. For example, Judges 3 shows how He chose to test His children in the Promised Land by leaving ungodly peoples for them to battle, "to teach warfare to the descendants of the Israelites who had not had previous battle experience" (v. 2).

Through the several clear examples recorded, many battle strategies are revealed. The children of Israel were doing evil in God's eyes as they dwelt among wicked peoples. This resulted in their being sold into the hand of the king of Mesopotamia for eight years (see v. 8).

However, when they cried out to the Lord for deliverance, He sent Caleb's little brother, Othniel, to deliver them (see v. 9). The tribes of Israel fought against the ruthless king's army, and with God's power were victorious, so that *"the land had peace for forty years"* (v. 11).

They fell into this pattern again and again. Over and over they perpetuated the cycle of sin, bondage, oppression, turning to the Lord, and deliverance. For instance, another time when they turned away and resumed their wickedness, God "gave them into the hands of the Midianites" for seven years (6:1). Year after year these fierce marauders pillaged Israel's vineyards and fields; year after year the Israelites cowered in terror.

Again the cries of God's people were directed to heaven and were heard.

> Midian so impoverished the Israelites that they cried out to the LORD for help. When the Israelites cried to the LORD because of Midian, he sent them a prophet, who said, "This is what the LORD, the God of Israel, says: I brought you up out of Egypt, out of the land of slavery. I snatched you from the power of Egypt and from the hand of all your oppressors. I drove them from before you and gave you their land. I said to you, 'I am the LORD your God; do not worship the gods of the Amorites, in whose land you live.' But you have not listened to me" (Judges 6:6–10).

Gideon, a common and simple but consecrated young man, was selected as the people's deliverer after the prophet revealed the Lord's response.

When Gideon was in the field threshing wheat, minding his own business, an angel of the Lord appeared to him and said, *"The LORD is with you, mighty warrior"* (v. 12). In my paraphrase, Gideon said, "You've got to be kidding—*me*?! My family is poor and powerless, and I'm the weakest of us all."

13

Accepting no excuses, God's angel insisted that Gideon would be the leader to prevail against the oppressors and lead the people into battle to achieve a full victory. While he was the leader, "the land enjoyed peace forty years" (8:28), and Israel therein learned new (but timeless) battle strategies.

* * *

If you too are called to learn the lessons of battle, know that there are at least three essential "musts" of leadership in spiritual warfare:

(1) You must receive the assignment from God. (6:12)

(2) You must consent to God's call. (vv. 22–24)

(3) You must always operate under the control of God's Spirit. (v. 34)

Furthermore, the Word reveals another crucial truth: The first step of effective warfare is to "cry out to the Lord."

Second, we know spiritual warfare exists for the same reason we know electricity (also invisible) exists—*we experience it.* There's evidence of the battle all around us. There are victims and victors. The effects are measurable.

I'm reminded of the little boy who asked his father how wars begin.

"Well," said his father, "suppose that America quarreled with England."

"But," interrupted the mother, "America mustn't quarrel with England."

"I know," he answered; "but I'm talking hypothetically."

"You are misleading the child," said the mother.

"I am not," he answered.

"You are too."

"No I'm not!"

"Yes you are!"

"All right, Dad," said the small boy, "I think I know how wars begin now."[1]

In his wonderful book *Journey to the Mountain of God*, David Ireland writes:

> When I became a Christian, I had never before heard the term *spiritual warfare*. I thought that praying the Sinner's Prayer assured me of heaven *and* of a problem-free life on earth. I soon found out that a dreaded enemy of God and of God's people existed named Satan. He does not want God's purposes to be satisfied in my life or in yours. Peter told the Jewish Christian community: "Be self-controlled and alert. Your enemy the devil prowls around like a roaring lion looking for someone to devour. Resist him, standing firm in faith, because you know that your brothers throughout the world are undergoing the same kind of sufferings" (1 Peter 5:8–9).
>
> Peter identified Satan as our enemy. Forget the happy-go-lucky attitude that pursuing God is all about worship and praise. Pursuing God includes learning how to fight and win![2]

THE SPIRITUAL

The word *spiritual* can throw us off. Because it's *spiritual* warfare, some of us confuse it with spiritual maturity. Some feel that if they can master the skills of spiritual warfare they will be spiritually mature. This isn't the case.

Spiritual warfare is not synonymous with spiritual maturity. A new believer, though spiritually immature, may be thrust by the

Spirit of God into spiritual battle with little preparation. If and when this happens, God will provide the necessary authority and direction.

Spiritual *maturity* and *discernment* come from years of loving God and living for Him, from faithfully walking with and serving Him. Spiritual maturity is a result of our rightly applying God's Word, standing firm in the faith, and repeatedly overcoming the enemy (see Hebrews 5:14).

There are immature Christians who are attracted to spiritual warfare to the degree that they become "addicted" to it. It's all they think of night and day, and they get so caught up that they *spiritualize* everything. Some foolishly become superstitious and routinely feel compelled to invest meaning into every physical thing. To hear them you'd think that every storm that appears is demonically inspired, or else it carries a divine purpose. Sadly many of their conclusions are entirely explainable by natural conditions and are more a product of lively imagination than of true spiritual discernment. In time, with loving leadership, they can grow in spiritual discernment and accuracy. They will also learn how and when to share their insights.

* * *

Now, don't get me wrong. I would be foolish to suggest that the devil doesn't rile up the waters. One night as Jesus sailed across the Sea of Galilee, He approached the territory held captive by the Gadarene demoniac, who was host to a legion of demons. (A "legion," militarily, was a regiment of about *five thousand* soldiers.)

When Jesus and His disciples encountered a sudden storm, everyone was disturbed except Him. He knew the assignment His Father had given was to go to Gadara, and He knew He would see victory. Jesus, our mighty battle strategist, commanded the winds to stop, and they did. The stunned disciples exclaimed, "Wow! Did you see that? Who *is* this? *Everything* answers to him. Cool!" (my paraphrase; see Mark 4:35–5:15). Upon arrival, Jesus cast out the legion of demons and set the demoniac free. This power encounter shook up the entire territory.

Physical things can indeed represent spiritual reality, as Moses' bronze snake on the pole represented life and healing to the snake-bitten children of Israel (see Numbers 21:8–9). But some Christians seem, willy-nilly, to attribute spiritual significance to anything and everything. They view their car's transmission failure and their lost earring as *acts of war against them* by Satan.

That's not to say demonic forces never cause such things; rather, they aren't always the cause. To think otherwise is to over-spiritualize. For instance, if it isn't given proper and consistent maintenance, a car ultimately will break down with or without the devil.

I know how tempting it can be to make assumptions! Like when I've had serious computer problems while writing an article or book about warfare. However, I must remember that unless I've left him an "open door" of access—say, unconfessed sin or an unholy alliance—the enemy must have God's permission before he can touch me or my stuff. John, the beloved disciple, wrote: "We know that anyone born of God does not continue to sin; the one who was born of God keeps him safe, and the evil one cannot harm him" (1 John 5:18).

One night I was working on just such an article. The morning and afternoon had been challenging, filled with office needs and schedule pressures. My deadline was approaching, but my presentation wasn't coming together. I was anxious and frustrated.

At one point earlier in the day I'd spoken rudely to my wife,

Alice, but I hadn't considered it any further. Now, sitting at my computer with my fingers on the keyboard, awaiting inspiration, I stopped to pray: "Lord, I need your help. Show me what to do."

Right away I remembered how I had treated Alice. Convicted, I went and apologized. After a kiss and a hug, I returned to the task, and, like liquid gold, the anointing of the Lord poured over me to finish the article.

In this case, God was allowing the frustration and discomfort to instruct and test me. A good teacher examines his or her students, and God, the best teacher, is no exception.

THE WARFARE

Warfare implies a battle, doesn't it? But what *about* the battle? Who are the combatants, and why are they at odds?

Some of us see the devil primarily as *our* enemy—ours personally. To hear them, you'd think Satan himself is entirely immersed in plotting and planning strategies against them and their concerns. That's hardly likely, however, because Satan has limited power, limited knowledge, and can be only one place at a time. As currently there are more than six and a half billion people on earth, I doubt he has any idea who or where I am.

You and I aren't Satan's primary enemies. We arrived on the scene a few thousand years too late. He was at war with our Father eons before we came along. And here we discover the only reason he even messes with us—he hates our Heavenly Daddy!

This timeless cosmic conflict into which we were born is between God and Satan. We were born on a battlefield in the midst of war; one of the warring parties is our Father, which highlights the part we play in combat.

Perhaps it would help to put this in context. Rebecca Greenwood writes in *Authority to Tread:*

> The day John baptized Jesus in the Jordan River was the day of an invasion so great that, by comparison, it could make D-Day of World War II seem like a mere video game. From that day on, Jesus and His disciples began preaching the Gospel of the Kingdom of God.
>
> A "kingdom" by definition, has a government headed up by a king. Jesus was the invading King. The kingdom He was invading also had a government, and its king was Satan. For thousands of years after the time of Adam and Eve, the human population of the whole world, with a few exceptions, such as the people of God in Israel, was under the evil control of the prince of the power of the air. Practically speaking, Satan could do anything he wanted to the peoples of the earth. And what he did was not good.
>
> Things radically changed when God sent His Son. From the time of Jesus until now, the war has been hot and it is getting hotter. The Kingdom of God has been advancing as it always has advanced—namely by force (see Matthew 11:12). Satan's fury continues to swell because he knows his time is shorter than it ever has been.[3]

We were born sinners, and, in time, given the freedom to choose, every one of us chose sin and proved our lost condition. We once were known as children of Satan (see 1 John 3:10; yikes, that hurts!). Knowing that God's purposes are all wrapped up with His desire for spiritual children, don't you imagine Satan basked in the thought that he had gained custody of even one whom God had created to be His child?

Billions of people around the world suffer from satanic domination of their lives. Turn on the news anytime, and it's more murder, rape, abuse, abortion, and violence. We were miserably lost when God found us. Had He not, we might have been tonight's featured tragedy on *Headline News*, and in the end we would have been cast into the hell God prepared for the devil and his angels (not for people; see Matthew 25:41).

* * *

Only my oldest and closest friends know that one of my hobbies once was ventriloquism. As a young evangelist I had several ventriloquist figures and used them in skits to present the gospel to children and teens. Years later, after I stopped traveling and became a pastor, I began carving figures again. I made them with eyebrows that would rise, eyes that would look left and right, a hand that would extend. I enjoyed creating and selling them.

Several more years later, I was driving past a garage sale when from the corner of my eye I saw something familiar. One of my figures was for sale. I stopped quickly, jumped out, and ran to purchase it before someone else did. It was such a prize for me. After all, I'd created it myself. Now it was twice mine—I made it, *and* I bought it!

This analogy resembles our relationship with the Father. Again, we were born sinners, and soon thereafter proved our condition by submitting to sin. We were lost and for sale on Satan's auction block. But Jesus paid the price for our redemption, bought us back with great joy, and took us home with Him!

Today God is carefully "carving us" into the likeness of His Son (see Romans 8:29). Impossible? No, because when God saved us, Christ came to live by His Spirit in us, and Christ in us is the very hope of glory. What an indescribably amazing plan!

The Lord has ransomed us from our slavery to sin. He has set up His kingdom *in* us so He can extend His kingdom *through* us (see Luke 17:21). As we share the saving gospel of Christ with others, He transforms life after life, nation after nation, ultimately to fill His heavenly house with children.

It's the ultimate *viral* experience. He who had only one begotten Son now has billions of kids! The primary purpose for *everything* is to satisfy the Father-heart of God.

INSIGHTS TO REMEMBER

- Spiritual warfare is real, and it's a real war.
- We shouldn't become "addicted" to warfare and begin to spiritualize everything in life.
- Physical things and experiences can represent spiritual reality.
- God will *allow* the enemy to frustrate and discomfit us, to teach and test us.
- God is Satan's primary enemy.
- Although we are created in God's image, our sin caused us to become lost.
- God saves us to set up His kingdom in us and extend it through us.

CHAPTER 2

THE SATANIC STRATEGY

The old country church was having a revival meeting the last week of October, which meant it coincided with Halloween.

In that neighborhood was a group of teens with a wild streak. They had decided to dress up in costume, go trick-or-treating with the younger children, and see if any adventure turned up.

Of course this grew old quickly, and at that point they were like the atheist who died—all dressed up with nowhere to go. So they picked a place: They decided they'd go spook the revival gathering.

When the kids arrived at the church, they each took up a position at one of the doors or windows. On a given command, they barged in on the evangelist's message and yelled *"BOO!"*

The parishioners were paralyzed with shock.

Jimmy, wearing an improvised "devil's suit," had jumped through the front door near the piano. Holding up his arms threateningly, he now crept slowly toward the front row . . . and toward elderly Sister Churchgoer, who hadn't missed a Sunday in decades and wore the perfect-attendance pins to prove it.

The aged spinster, terrified, began shaking like a leaf. As Jimmy came almost nose to nose with her, she said, "Now you *listen*, Mister Devil. I've been a member at this here church for thirty-five years!" Then, in a lower tone, hand cupped over her mouth, she whispered, "But I've been on *your* side all the time."

SATAN'S ORIGIN

Satan didn't begin as an evil creature. He may well have been a scary creature nonetheless. He was an anointed cherub. And believe me, a cherub is no "chubby baby angel" as, over the centuries, the renderings of European artists may have led us to believe.

In fact, 1 Kings 6:26 says the two golden cherubs made to arch over the ark of the covenant were ten cubits high; that's fifteen to sixteen feet tall! No wonder that almost every time people in Scripture met an angel face-to-face they, like Spinster Churchgoer, were terrified. Satan must have been an awesome, glorious creature. Originally God created him to serve, and named him Lucifer ("shining one").

Some refer to Lucifer as an archangel. Michael (whose name means "Who is like God?") is the only angel identified in Scripture as an archangel (see Jude 9); Gabriel (whose name means "God is mighty") also is thought to be an archangel. Various theologians suggest that Lucifer was the highest of God's creation before humankind was made; if that's true, our sudden appearance on the scene certainly could have provided him reason to envy us, created in God's own image. Lucifer, now Satan, perhaps saw us as having robbed him of highly coveted divine favor.

It's commonly thought that Gabriel serves the Holy Spirit and His purposes, that Michael serves the Father and His purposes, and that Lucifer was created to serve the Son and His purposes. If this is actually the case, these three angels were like "personal assistants" to the Trinity.

Scripture suggests that Lucifer was heaven's worship leader. God's judgment of the wicked king of Tyre, in Ezekiel 28:12–15, also seemingly refers to Lucifer's rebellion and judgment, speaking of an "anointed cherub" who God set on His "holy mountain" (v. 14). Ezekiel mentions his having been in the garden of Eden; also, he was perfect, before he sinned. Of course, none of these things refer to a mere man (e.g., the king of Tyre). Let's read the passage.

> Son of man, take up a lamentation upon the king of Tyrus, and say unto him, Thus saith the Lord GOD; Thou sealest up the sum, full of wisdom, and perfect in beauty.
>
> *Thou hast been in Eden the garden of God*; every precious stone was thy covering, the sardius, topaz, and the diamond, the beryl, the onyx, and the jasper, the sapphire, the emerald, and the carbuncle, and gold: the workmanship of *thy tabrets* and of *thy pipes* was prepared in thee in the day that thou wast created.
>
> Thou art the anointed *cherub* that covereth; and I have set thee so: *thou wast upon the holy mountain of God*; thou hast walked up and down in the midst of the stones of fire.
>
> *Thou wast perfect* in thy ways from the day that thou wast created, till iniquity was found in thee. (KJV, emphasis mine)

The conclusion that Lucifer was heaven's worship leader is based primarily on the words *tabrets*, *pipes*, and *cherub*.

The Hebrew word translated *tabrets* means "tambourine," which has an obvious musical connotation. The term translated *pipes*, however, carries no musical connotation; it doesn't, as some have thought, refer to flutes, trumpets, pipe organs, or any other wind instrument. It literally means "bezel," a metal setting into which a precious stone is set for display. This isn't surprising, since in Ezekiel the word follows a list of precious stones.

The third word, *cherub*, is intriguing, for here Lucifer is referred to as "the anointed cherub that covereth." What was he to cover? C. I. Scofield suggests that Lucifer's job was to cover the earth with light, since he was the angel of light. At his fall, all light left him, leaving the possibility of Genesis 1:2, which says the surface of the earth was covered with darkness.

While certain aspects of this might be in the realm of mystery or speculation, I believe Lucifer originally led the innumerable angelic beings in passionate worship of Jehovah God, on His holy mountain, for His glory; Ezekiel 28 is a sad song, a lament over the iniquity found in Lucifer and over his ultimate fall.

Allow me to imagine for a moment. Perhaps one day Lucifer shifted out of worship mode and caught a glimpse of the selfless, wholehearted devotion God's heavenly beings offered Him, and envy took root in his heart. He no longer wanted to prompt their worship of the Almighty but to receive it for himself.

At that moment sin was found in Lucifer; no longer fit for heaven, he was cast into the earth. Job 41:33–34 says,

Nothing on earth is his equal—
    a creature without fear.
He looks down on all that are haughty;
    he is king over all that are proud.

John Milton said Lucifer preferred being king of hell to being a servant of heaven.

When I've taught on this subject and say, "No longer fit for heaven, Lucifer was cast into . . .?" there is almost always a corporate answer: "hell." It's true that hell is his *final* home. But until now, Satan still roams back and forth *in the earth* (see Job 2:1–2 and Revelation 12:9).

* * *

When was he cast out of heaven? That's a mystery. Possibly he was cast out before Genesis 1, which, after all, speaks of the earth being without form and void, and darkness covering the face of the deep (v. 2). This suggests God created the earth and whatever life He put on it, *then* it became void and covered with darkness, *then* "God said, 'Let there be light,' and there was light" (v. 3).

From there, God didn't create the earth again; He populated it. We don't know for sure what the earth was *before* it became void and covered with darkness. According to this idea, when Satan and his fallen angels were cast into the earth, the darkness appeared. Then God said, "Let there be light."

Some suggest Lucifer fell at the moment Jesus said, "I saw Satan fall like lightning from heaven" (Luke 10:18). Still others believe that Satan's fall is yet in the future!

All things considered, it appears to me that Lucifer and his angels fell from heaven prior to the Genesis creation account. Otherwise, how would he have appeared as the serpent in the garden of Eden?

When Satan arrived on planet earth isn't important, though. Fact is, he's here.

Satanic Pseudonyms

Satan's names are many. Here are a few.

- The god of this world ("age"; 2 Corinthians 4:4)
- The prince of the power of the air (Ephesians 2:2 KJV; "The ruler of the kingdom of the air" NIV)
- The tempter (1 Thessalonians 3:5)
- The devil (1 Timothy 3:6–7)
- The serpent; the dragon (Genesis 3; Revelation 12:3–4; 13:4)
- The deceiver (implied; Revelation 20:3)
- The evil one (John 17:15; 1 John 5:19)
- Satan (Zechariah 3:1; Revelation 12:9)
- An angel of light (2 Corinthians 11:14)
- A liar/the father of lies (John 8:44)
- A roaring lion (1 Peter 5:8)
- The thief (John 10:10)
- The leviathan (Job 41)
- Beelzebub (Matthew 12:27)

THE REBELLION

One-third of heaven's angels revolted with Lucifer; God cast them out of heaven and into the earth. Once here, Lucifer's name was changed to Satan ("the accuser"), and he also is called the devil ("the deceiver"). He witnessed the creations of light, nature, and humankind (see Genesis 1:1–2:7). He is worshiped by billions of people around the world, some directly, most indirectly. A few worship his actual personage; he seduces the overwhelming majority to worship nature, a religious figure, or gods of their own making. He and his minions are the power behind *every* false god.

International evangelist Morris Cerullo makes a great point, one that, as with cherubs (see above), debunks a myth largely born of Renaissance art and bearing no resemblance to reality:

> Everyone has seen the caricatures which depict Satan with pointed ears and tail, dressed in a red suit, with a wicked gleam in his eye and a pitchfork in his hand. Nothing could be further from the truth.[1]

Satan is horrifically cruel, an unimaginably devious enemy with extensive understanding of warfare strategy. Don't ever lose sight of that. He's brilliant and seductive. Don't think he can't seduce you; his ability to seduce explains why we're such sinners. He seduced countless leagues of angels to rebel against and turn their back upon God, serving falsehood instead. Those who followed him also fell with him—we refer to them as fallen angels.

Most who've studied these matters maintain that the fallen angels are what today we call demons. However, other scholars believe the term *fallen angels* applies only to the prince demons that rule territories from the heavenlies (see chapter 7). They maintain that run-of-the-mill, ground-level, everyday demons are not fallen angels at all but something else altogether (see chapter 5).

If only the upper-level territorial rulers are fallen angels, then what are the demons that seek to inhabit human bodies, as in the case of demonized people?

I don't consider this to be worth arguing about, but I am willing to explain why I don't necessarily believe earthbound demons are fallen angels.

- There isn't a biblical case in which an angel sought a body to inhabit. When an angel appeared, he appeared in bodily form. Angels have bodies (e.g., see Genesis 19; Matthew 28:1–7).
- There's no indication that the fallen angels lost their angelic bodies when they were cast out of heaven.
- In 2 Kings 19:35, we read of one angel singlehandedly killing *185,000* Assyrian soldiers. And yet after almost forty years of deliverance ministry that has involved thousands of demonic encounters throughout the nations of the world, I've never yet discovered a demon that frightened me (not that they haven't tried). So I believe demons are something other than fallen angels.

Chuck Swindoll once said,

I like Gary Larsen's cartoon, *The Far Side*. He had a cartoon once that showed a guy looking real slick, with his sleeves rolled up. He's got an incredible hairdo. His tie is pulled loose. He's holding a vacuum cleaner. In line are people with a television set, a toaster, and another appliance. And he says to the vacuum cleaner, with his hands on it, "I command the foul demons that have clogged this vacuum cleaner to come out." It struck me funny. But I'm not making light of demons; I'm making light of sensationalism.[2]

Seriously, demons likely are either (1) the spirits of a pre-Adamic race of beings or (2) the spirits of the Nephilim—unruly, gigantic men who were the offspring of "the sons of God" and human women (see Genesis 6).

Why would this be true?

- Who would want a human body to inhabit more than someone who once had one?

- Demons seek to satisfy their wicked desires through access to a human body.

- Say there was indeed a pre-Adamic race that walked the earth *before* it "became void, and darkness covered the face of the deep," before the giving of light. They wouldn't be the offspring (seed) of Adam, the father of humankind, who opened the door to sin in our race. So they wouldn't be included in the work of Christ, the second Adam's atoning sin-payment at Calvary. No hope of heaven.

- If this is true, then their bodies eventually died, and their spirits, ever since, have wandered the earth looking to hijack physical bodies in which to dwell.

These statements perhaps could also be made of the Nephilim (Hebrew word for *giant,* literally meaning "fallen ones"; see Genesis 6), for although they were born of women, they had no human fathers. They were produced by angelic beings—"the sons of God." They wouldn't have been covered under the Lord's sacrificial saving grace either. Thus it's reasonable to assume that their spirits likewise would thirst for a body to inhabit.

Furthermore, it makes sense that they would be angry with us—the recipients of God's grace and of Christ's atoning blood, destined for heavenly eternity in His presence. And it explains other things, like why these beings would seek to drive a person to commit suicide (kill his or her own body).

Anyway, though, since none of us knows for sure the source or origin of demons, the issue is not something on which we should get hung up. The point is, they're here and they must be dealt with.

THE STAKES

From the moment God created humankind in His image, Satan has competed with Him for our obedience, devotion, and worship. Satan, who *isn't* omnipresent, moves throughout the earth looking for people he can devour (see 1 Peter 5:8). He seeks to influence and then rule individuals, and then to take dominion over territories and nations and all the people therein. Scripture describes him as the god of this world (i.e., of this "world system"; see 2 Corinthians 4:4).

Satan is in a predicament. He's fighting a war he can't win, against an enemy (Jehovah God) he can't defeat. God could annihilate Satan with less than the blink of an eye, yet Satan cannot kill or harm God at all. God allows Satan limited reign for now because in a strange way he still is fulfilling God's purposes for the ages.

One purpose Satan fulfills is that of testing us. And this he does quite well. God *allows* him to test us, but not to see if we will pass or fail; God already knows. He allows the devil's testing to strengthen us and to prepare us for fruitful service regardless of any satanic onslaught. When Jesus told Peter that Satan was about to sift him, He added, *"But I've prayed for you"* (Luke 22:31–32).

Jesus could have prayed that the Father would prevent Satan from sifting Peter. But no—He prayed that Satan's testing would strengthen Peter so that he likewise would be able to strengthen others. Here's that viral thing again. Today, thousands of years later, *we* are strengthened by the experiences of Peter, Job, Paul, and many others.

Have you noticed that it was *God's* idea for Satan to sift Job?

> One day when the angels came to report to GOD, Satan also showed up. GOD singled out Satan, saying, "And what have you been up to?" Satan answered God, "Oh, going here and there, checking things out."
>
> *Then God said to Satan, "Have you noticed my friend Job? There's no one quite like him, is there—honest and true to his word, totally devoted to God and hating evil? He still has a firm grip on his integrity! You tried to trick me into destroying him, but it didn't work."*
>
> Satan answered, "A human would do anything to save his life. But what do you think would happen if you reached down and took away his health? He'd curse you to your face, that's what."
>
> *God said, "All right. Go ahead—you can do what you like with him. But mind you, don't kill him."*
>
> Satan left God and struck Job with terrible sores. Job was ulcers and scabs from head to foot. They itched and oozed so badly that he took a piece of broken pottery to scrape himself, then went and sat on a trash heap, among the ashes. (Job 2:1–8 THE MESSAGE, emphasis mine. This was only the *beginning* of Job's trials.)

THE GOAL: BEING NEITHER FOOLISH NOR FEARFUL

There are two views of Satan that concern me. One is the idea that because we are victorious in Christ, we can belittle the devil, calling him names and taunting him, and so on. Friend, that attitude exposes an ignorance of the ethics of war. Allow me to explain: When an army captures a high-level enemy officer, they treat him with a level of respect that's above the way they treat other captives. At this point in human history, more people on earth worship Satan (in his various forms) than worship God. Peter alludes to the importance of recognizing this.

> Keep a cool head. Stay alert. The Devil is poised to pounce,
> and would like nothing better than to catch you napping.
> (1 Peter 5:8 THE MESSAGE)

I heard two preachers arguing one day. The first, bringing correction to the other for calling Satan silly names, said, "I wouldn't belittle Satan that way. Even Michael the archangel didn't ridicule Satan in their Jude 9 encounter."

The other preacher said, "Nor would I if I were *only* an archangel. I'm a blood-bought, born-again child of God, with royal blood flowin' in my veins."

Forgive me, but I think if he were dying, that man would gladly take a blood transfusion from anyone. At any rate, he was missing the point.

So I'm concerned for those of us who seem unable to show appropriate respect for our adversary. Second, I'm equally concerned for those who apparently attribute sovereignty to Satan. In Revelation 20, we read about one angel (not identified as an archangel) who binds Satan with a chain—for a thousand years! The truth is that a toddler, commanded and commissioned by God and given a chain to do so, could bind Satan.

Those who over-esteem the devil apparently have overlooked Jesus' *allowing* Satan to sift Peter, and the Father's *suggesting* to Satan that he test Job. Have they lost sight of the fact that Satan is

God's devil, "on God's leash"? God can jerk that leash anytime He chooses. It must infuriate the devil to discover that after he's done his best work . . . he's still as damned as ever, and in truth he has only succeeded in helping God accomplish His purposes!

As for us, once we're reborn, God uses even our sinful past for His glory (see Romans 8:28). But *don't* consider this a free pass to continue living out the sins of your past. The apostle Paul makes it clear that our liberty in Christ is not for the purpose of wrong-doing but for the purpose of victory (see Romans 6:15–23).

Yes, God forgives sin. Yes, God works together "all things" in our past for good. Our past sin *won't* bring eternal death, because of Christ's shed blood; nevertheless, the effects of that sin still bear evidence. Perhaps this brief old story clearly illustrates.

> A farmer had a son. As his son grew into his teens, he would be occasionally disobedient. When his son sinned, the father would take him to the barn door, give him a hammer and a nail, and insist that he pound a nail into the door.
>
> Over time, the door became filled with nails. At the right time, the father took his son to the barn to teach him an important life lesson.
>
> He handed his son the hammer and instructed him to pull each nail out of the door, and, as he did, to thank God for forgiving the sin it represented.
>
> When it was finished he said, "Now, son, don't you feel better?"
>
> His son agreed that he did.
>
> "Is there anything left on the door?"
>
> The son said, "No, sir."
>
> "Look again," the father encouraged.
>
> It was then that the son discovered that although the nails (sins) were gone, the door was filled with nail holes . . . holes that would remain.

Even though where sin abounds, God's grace much more abounds, we do not consider this a license to sin. Although sins can be forgiven and the nails removed, their results can remain catastrophic—we see this, for example, in the destruction of marriages and the ruination of Christian testimonies.

In almost fifty years of ministry, I've had many believers ask me to pray for their deliverance from life's "sifting circumstances." However, I've yet to have one being sifted with sickness, sadness, or betrayal ask me to pray that they will be strengthened by the sifting! People have elevated *being delivered from* circumstances over *being developed by* them.

I'm convinced that many Christians who attribute sovereignty to Satan suffer from anxiety and other negative emotional/physical symptoms for fear of what he might do to them next. They've yet to learn that they are Christ's; He lives in them, and they live in Him.

I've never awakened in the middle of the night wondering what sinister plan the devil is concocting that's going to catch God (my Father) off guard. "Oops" is not a word in heaven's vocabulary! God has conquered Satan. And God says that the Greater One lives in me (see 1 John 4:4).

God, not Satan, is in control of history. And yes, to some degree, Satan and his demons still serve the Most High God. How do we know? Because were it otherwise, God could remove them all with a divine sneeze.

* * *

When I was a young minister in the mid-1960s, I worked on Sunset Strip in Hollywood. That's right: I worked on the most "hip" street in America. We had a small office across the street from

Deano's nightclub, the building that provided the backdrop for the TV series *77 Sunset Strip*. Remember teen idol Edd "Kookie" Byrnes and his pocket comb? Are you too old to remember? Or too young to know what I'm talking about? Just kidding—actually, Deano's, like our office, was in the 6500 block of the Strip in West Hollywood, not 7700.

Nightly we would teach, and then we'd lead a group of Christians out street-witnessing. Let me tell you, my experiences there would make a fascinating book. On a given weekend night, I'd pass out more than five hundred gospel tracts and witness to dozens of people, both in the clubs and on the streets. It was the height of the hippie revolution, and the Strip was jam-packed with them all night long.

After a couple years of this, I was invited to a large church in Alabama for a revival meeting. Its pastor had married my parents and was one of their closest friends. So it wasn't a complete surprise when, at the end of the event, he said, "Eddie, I want to offer you a job on my staff. Go back home to California, pack your stuff in a trailer, and head this way. I'll present the issue to the church on Wednesday night and they'll be thrilled. We'll cover your moving costs. Understand that in my twenty-seven years here as pastor, they've never voted against anything I've proposed. Welcome aboard!"

Wow! I was *excited*. The salary was much more than I currently was receiving; this was a mega-church in its day. In the plane, on the way home, I was already decorating my office in my mind.

On Monday, I loaded up my U-Haul in Hollywood and joyfully headed toward Birmingham.

I made it to Houston by Wednesday afternoon and decided to

stay overnight in a hotel. I thought I'd also check in with my "new boss," so later that evening I called him at home.

"Pastor, how did it go tonight?" I asked, animated.

"Who is this?" he replied.

"Pastor, this is Eddie."

"Eddie who?"

At that point I knew I was in trouble. "This is Eddie Smith, and I'm calling to ask how the church felt about my coming aboard."

"Oh . . . Brother Eddie. Uh . . . I . . . I mentioned hiring you to my deacons at our monthly meeting Monday night, and . . . ah . . . they don't feel it's a good time for us to be bringing on another staff member."

Of course, my heart dropped. "Pastor, I went back to California and packed everything I own into a trailer; I've driven two days, and I'm in Texas tonight on my way to Birmingham. Last week, you agreed to cover my moving costs. I don't have the money to pay for the gasoline, the motel, or the trailer rental. What are you going to do?"

"Well, since you're not coming here now, we won't be able to help you with that, but God bless you, son. Good night!"

I was stunned. Call it a betrayal, a test, a sifting . . . all I knew was, I was heartbroken and broke in Houston.

I won't share the details of God's guidance and provision, but I will tell you this: Had I not suffered that disappointment, I would never have been in Houston, Texas. Had I not been in Houston, I would not have met my precious wife, Alice. And . . . you get the point. No matter what the world or the devil throws at us, God works it all together "for the good of those who love him, who have been called according to his purpose" (Romans 8:28).

INSIGHTS TO REMEMBER

- Satan (Lucifer) was once a magnificent and beautiful cherub—possibly heaven's worship leader.

- Sin entered Satan's heart, and he was cast into the earth.

- Satan seduced one-third of heaven's angels to rebel with him.

- Some believe the fallen angels are now ground-level demons.

- Others believe the fallen angels to be high-level principalities.

- Satan competes with God for our worship.

- Satan, although filled with hatred for God, mysteriously still serves God's purposes.

- Satan must have God's permission to move against us.

- Sometimes, as with Job, Satan's movement against us is part of God's plan to develop our Christlikeness.

CHAPTER 3

THE ENEMY'S TARGETS

Satan is fully aware of Scripture, and he clearly knows that in the end his defeat will be both final and eternal. Like a condemned prisoner on death row, he's been judged, found guilty, condemned to hell, and is now waiting for the sentence to be carried out (see Matthew 25:41; Revelation 20:10). Satan knows in his head that God has prepared hell for him and his followers. Yet in his heart he still hopes he will be released and escape eternal punishment. It's *hope* that keeps him pressing on.

Crazy, isn't it? But billions of lost people have received enough revelation to cling to the same false comfort. They're hell-bound, yet they *hope* to make it to heaven. We hear it all the time: "I just hope the good things I've done will outweigh the bad." (As if God has a set of giant scales we'll all be weighed upon.) Or, "I feel like I'm as good as most churchgoers I know." Thankfully, unlike Satan, for whom there is no hope, as long as man has breath he has hope—assuming we take seriously our responsibility to share the gospel of Christ.

In the meantime Satan, an egomaniacal tyrant blinded by pride and hatred, works night and day to thwart God's plan. But his weapons aren't aimed at God at all. Remember, Satan can't hurt God directly, so he aims his weapons at us. *We are his targets!* This explains the answer to the question, "If God is Satan's enemy, why is Satan shooting at *me*?"

THE TACTICS

In my book *How to Be Heard in Heaven,*[1] I present three ways that Satan can hurt Jehovah. And all three have to do with God's ultimate purpose of being a loving Father.

Blinding the Lost

First, Satan blinds the minds of lost people with a spiritual veil so they cannot receive the gospel revelation necessary for them to become God's children. This hurts God, whose desire is to father His kids and have a houseful of children for eternity.

When we pray for the lost, it's important that we consider this "spiritual veil." Unless we do, winning them to Christ will be like trying to show a blind man a highway sign.

* * *

I'm reminded of one snowy day in beautiful Riga, Latvia. Our mission team had spent three hours sharing the gospel and discussing our countries' cultural differences in a large elementary school. The outside temperature, considering the wind-chill factor, felt close to zero degrees Fahrenheit, and there was at least a foot of snow on the ground.

The teachers and students wore their heavy coats, scarves, hats, and gloves *inside the building* because the city hadn't paid Russia for fuel oil, and they had none with which they could heat the school. What's more, there was no hot water anywhere in town. I was so cold my goose bumps had their own goose bumps.

After the assembly program, we headed for the exit, eager to find a warmer place. But we were stopped at the door by two teachers and their principal, who insisted that we stay for refreshments in their lounge. As badly as we wanted to return to the relative warmth of our hotel, coffee did sound good, so we agreed.

We watched one of the ladies prepare coffee and snacks while we chatted through our interpreter with the other two. She used no filter or coffeemaker. She simply poured grounds into a pot of boiling water and let it simmer a few minutes, Latvian-style. Then she filled our cups with coffee (and yes, a few grounds as well).

Our snacks were quite good. We were impressed and grateful for their hospitality and thoughtfulness; the Latvians are gracious people. They showered us with bouquets of flowers the entire time we were there.

Before we left the school, I asked the teachers if I could pray for them. They agreed, so I offered a rather typical American farewell prayer, adding my request for salvation and revival to be poured out on their village. I didn't bother to have it translated—I was freezing!

I'd no sooner finished when one of the teachers, a woman who looked to be in her mid-forties, said something to our translator. I inquired of her, and she explained, "Eddie, she said that you are a very powerful man."

This certainly got my attention. I joked, "My wife, Alice, is the only one who's ever mentioned that before." The Americans laughed politely.

"Ask her what she means," I pressed.

They exchanged a few Latvian words and then the interpreter switched back to English: "She said that a moment ago, while you were ending your prayer, something mysteriously broke off of her head and floated away."

"Tell her that God touched her. Ask her if she'd like Him to touch her again."

The interpreter did, and she nodded her approval.

"Ask her if I have permission to rest my hand on her shoulder while I pray for her." She agreed.

I laid my hand gently on her shoulder and prayed that God would open her heart to the revelation of Jesus. I repeated the gospel basics that she'd heard earlier, during our program, and then I asked if she was willing to repent of her sin and receive Christ as her Lord and Savior. Tears began to gently roll down her cheeks; she nodded affirmatively, and I led her in "the sinner's prayer."

When we finished, her weeping turned to tears of joy as she jumped from her chair, threw her head back, and began to dance joyfully around the room like a bird let free from its cage. She was elated.

I turned to the other teacher and asked if she'd also like to pray and receive Christ, having Him wash away her sins and then knowing that she'd spend eternity with Him in heaven.

She dropped her head, shrugged her shoulders, and mumbled something.

"What did she say?" I asked our interpreter.

She translated, "She said no—that she's 'a *quiet* woman.'"

I said, "Tell her that God loves His *quiet* daughters. Ask her if she'd like to be one."

The second she was told, she nodded.

With that, I led her through the same process. The moment we finished praying, she broke loose, grabbed the hands of the other teacher, and together they danced for joy. It was an amazing sight for our team to see.

Finally, I asked the principal if she wanted Christ to come into her heart. She stated she wasn't ready.

* * *

What broke off of the first teacher and floated away? The *spiritual veil* Satan puts on the minds of lost people to keep them from receiving the gospel revelation of salvation. The devil's deception prevents their being transferred from the kingdom of darkness into the kingdom of light.

So the first way Satan hurts God is by keeping the lost from being saved, robbing Him of children by reducing the number of souls in His kingdom.

Attacking the Family

A second way of hurting God is that the enemy *hurts us.* As loving parents of four remarkable children, I assure you that when any of them suffers, we suffer as well. There have been tearful times with each of our kids while trying to comfort them, when we too were brokenhearted. One of my dearest friends is watching her youngest son wrestle with cancer. I can't believe it's any less painful for her than for her sick son. When Satan hurts us, our Heavenly Daddy (*Abba*) feels our pain.

Years ago I counseled with a family that was having difficulty with their sixteen-year-old daughter. She was angry, rebellious, and wild. We struggled to reach a breakthrough before I discovered an awful fact.

More than sixteen years before, this couple had another teenage daughter who became pregnant outside of marriage. Pillars in their church and community, they were unwilling to bear their shame before friends and family. So they sent their daughter away to live with a friend in another city until she had delivered her beautiful baby girl.

During this time, the entire family moved to another town, where they now welcomed their daughter and her child. However, in the process, they plotted and schemed to tell their new friends and distant family that *they* were the baby's mother and father, and they allowed their daughter (the true mother) to be known as the baby's older sister. No one seemed to question the situation.

Bottom line: The baby was now a sixteen-year-old waiting in a nearby room, and they had never revealed to her that she was actually their *granddaughter* . . . and that her older sister was in reality her *mother*!

Immediately I saw the problem. The entire family was living a lie; this had opened the door for demonic activity; and demons usually take advantage by tormenting the weakest or most vulnerable family member—in this case, the teen.

I explained that they would eventually lose her unless they came clean, clearly explained, and repented for having lied to her for sixteen years. They struggled several minutes with the idea but finally agreed.

You can't imagine how shattered she was to learn the truth. It would have been one thing if she had been adopted and never told. That's a blow to many older children. But in this case, everything about her family relationships was based on lies. *Her big sister was her mom?!* It took quite a while to lead her to a place of peace, understanding, and forgiveness, and it wasn't easy.

* * *

There's something in that story you may have missed—I think we often miss it.

I've explained how these folks had sinned against their granddaughter. But I didn't mention how they had sinned against God. (We also had to deal with that.) *Our sin, any sin, is first and foremost a sin against our heavenly Father.*

Seducing the Children

Finally, the most diabolical way the devil hurts God is by *deceiving and luring us to sin, thereby wounding our Father.* No one can hurt me more deeply than my children can. When the neighbor's kids do something wrong it angers me. When my kids do something wrong it grieves me. *Grieve* is a love word. You can't grieve someone who doesn't love you. We can easily grieve the Holy Spirit, for instance (see Ephesians 4:30).

In the story I just shared, we see both. We can see how Satan lured the couple into lying to save face, and we can only imagine how much the pain their daughter and granddaughter experienced hurt the Lord. Like any loving father, when we hurt, He hurts (see Isaiah 53:3).

Furthermore, the enemy used the spiritual pride of this otherwise godly man and woman to injure the Father's heart. David the psalmist saw the results of this: "Against you [God], you only, have I sinned and done what is evil in your sight" (Psalm 51:4). We must never forget that sin will always take us further than we intended to go, keep us longer than we were planning to stay, and cost us more than we were prepared to pay.

* * *

Although we aren't the devil's primary enemy, he certainly is ours. And he'd like nothing more than to neutralize our witness, destroy our health, and entice us to dishonor Christ.

The first few years I was saved, I feared I'd do something wrong and God would hurt me. Now that I've walked with Him for more than sixty years, I realize the greater danger is that I'll do something wrong and hurt Him.

Ever since humankind was created, Satan has opposed us. He craves our destruction for many reasons, not the least of which is this: We were created to rule!

In his booklet *Strategies of Satan*, Morris Cerullo identifies nine warfare strategies Satan employs in this cosmic conflict. The devil strives to:

(1) Keep you in spiritual ignorance

(2) Make you believe he has unlimited power

(3) Make you believe he's more powerful than we (believers) are

(4) Make you believe that Christians should not face persecution

(5) Make you fall into a "spiritual sleep"

(6) Harden your heart against God

(7) Deceive you

(8) Use circumstances to defeat you

(9) Make you disobedient.[2]

Alice and I recently saw *Vantage Point,* a movie filled with action and suspense. I particularly liked a scene in which the life of the fictitious U.S. president was being threatened. An advisor, encouraging him to bomb a terrorist site in retaliation, says, "Mr. President, now is a time that we must act strong." He answers, "No. Now is a time when we must *be* strong."

That's my prayer for you!

INSIGHTS TO REMEMBER

- While God is Satan's enemy, we are Satan's targets.
- Satan hurts God by keeping men and women, boys and girls, *lost.*
- Satan hurts God by hurting God's children.
- Satan hurts God by luring us into sin, through which we grieve God.
- Satan hates us because we are God's children—destined for heaven, and created to rule!
- It's neither wise nor necessary to treat Satan disrespectfully.
- Sin, even when forgiven, does leave scars.

CHAPTER 4

THE ORIGINAL DESIGN

Had there been a newspaper in the garden that day, perhaps the *Eden Enquirer* headline would have been "MAN—Created to Rule!" God made every living thing for man's use and made him steward over it.

> Then God said, "Let us make man in our image, in our likeness, and let them rule over the fish of the sea and the birds of the air, over the livestock, over all the earth, and over all the creatures that move along the ground." So God created man in his own image, in the image of God he created him; male and female he created them. God blessed them and said to them, "Be fruitful and increase in number; fill the earth and subdue it. Rule over the fish of the sea and the birds of the air and over every living creature that moves on the ground" (Genesis 1:26–28).

Next, the Lord instructed Adam and Eve to be fruitful, to multiply, and to fill the earth with their children and their children's children—implying that their children were to also have dominion over creation. "The highest heavens belong to the LORD, but the earth he has given to man" (Psalm 115:16).

Adam and Eve were to care for the garden of Eden, the home God had made for them, with only one law to keep: "You must not eat of the tree of the knowledge of good and evil, for when you eat of it you will surely die" (Genesis 2:17).

One day Satan, the evil one disguised as a serpent, cleverly infiltrated God's glorious garden and challenged His integrity. He accused God of lying to Eve: "You won't die if you eat the forbidden fruit. God lied to you. He knows that if you eat that fruit you'll become a god, like Him!" (paraphrase of Genesis 3:4–5).

Furthermore, note an important distinction regarding Adam's authority. Adam was given rule over the plants and animals, *not over Eve.* Man wasn't created to rule men. *God* was to rule people, male and female; Adam and Eve and their children were simply to obey Him. Man ruling man is a result of sin (see v. 16); ever since the fall, Satan and his forces have used human rulers to control and bring misery to others.

ABDICATING THE THRONE

Adam and Eve defied God and thus produced the most tragic of headlines: "MAN RELINQUISHES RULE!" When Adam and Eve disobeyed God, they gave away their earthly rule to Satan, and, as Paul wrote, Satan became "the god of this age" (2 Corinthians 4:3–4). John would write, "The whole world is under the control of the evil one" (1 John 5:19). When Adam and Eve defied the Lord, sin entered the spiritual DNA of all humankind. From that point, anyone born of a human father would be prone to sin.

Thousands of years later, God clothed himself in human flesh in the womb of Mary, a teenage virgin (see Matthew 1:18). Fully God, Jesus is also fully man; on our behalf, He stepped out onto earth's stage to confront and overcome the devil as a human. Satan tempted Jesus by pointing to the world's kingdoms, ruled by man, and saying, "Jesus, if you will bow down and worship me, I'll give you the authority and splendor I've given these rulers, for it has been given to me. It's mine and I can give it to whomever I choose" (my paraphrase; see Luke 4).

Jesus didn't question or deny Satan's claim; He just turned down the offer. You see, in time, Father God will give the kingdoms of this world to His Son. Satan was offering Jesus *a shortcut*—one that would bypass the agonies of Calvary. However, the Master Strategist knew that if worshiping Satan was required to receive the kingdoms of men, then worshiping Satan would also be required to keep them.

The "Timeline" of Earthly Rule

- God creates, owns, and rules the world (see Psalm 24:1–2).
- God makes humankind to be its rulers (Genesis 1:26–28).
- Adam and Eve relinquish rule temporarily to Satan (Genesis 3:6).
- Satan expands his role and rules over fallen humanity (from the events of Genesis to the present day).
- Satan makes an offer to Christ; Christ rejects it (Luke 4:8).
- Christ defeats Satan at Calvary (John 19:30).
- Christ disarms Satan and regains rule (Colossians 2:15).

- Christ metes out rule (spiritual authority) to us, one assignment at a time, to confront satanic rule (Luke 10:19).

- Satan's ultimate and eternal defeat will be manifest in his everlasting punishment (Revelation 20:10).

Humankind (Adam and Eve) gave over earthly rule to Satan, a fallen angelic being. The spiritual warfare we do is the reversal of that transaction. This is the invisible power encounter between the kingdom of light and the kingdom of darkness. We are to preach the gospel of the kingdom throughout the earth (Matthew 24:14), completing the Great Commission (Matthew 28:19–20) and seeing the earth covered with the knowledge of God's glory (Habakkuk 2:14).

In spiritual warfare, believers who are indwelt, empowered, and directed by the Holy Spirit, force fallen angelic beings to relinquish their rule of the earth and of humanity through prayer, fasting, and exercising the authority of Christ and His cross.

SATAN'S GOAL IS NO SECRET

We know from John 10:10 that Satan is here to steal, to kill, and to destroy. But why? Because he hopes to one day rule the earth fully, receiving the worship of humans and angels. Simply put, Satan wants to *be* God (see Isaiah 14:14). I know, he said in his heart, "I will make myself *like* the Most High," but it's clear from the rest of his declarations that he plans to supplant God altogether (see chapter 6, "The Occult-Level Battlefield"). The devil wants us to marvel at his skill and cower in his presence. Don't do it!

He has organized his fallen angels to establish his hegemony. They have deceived the masses, and many of those he's duped have also been demonized—infiltrated, inspired, and supernaturally empowered by evil spirits. Some who are demonized hold positions of power in society's upper echelons; these are able to deceive and involve unsuspecting others. Many are "flying under the radar," to a point; others are overtly, blatantly evil.

Some are satanically skilled to rule territories. Others have little leadership skill, they're simply satanically empowered to rape, pillage, and plunder. Among these are mass murderers, pedophiles, and rapists. Many others are children and teens dabbling in the satanic, looking for supernatural power.

* * *

Several years ago a twenty-one-year-old Satanist came to me for counseling. When she walked into my office, the ambient temperature literally dropped several degrees. Swirling about her in the spirit realm, like a swarm of angry hornets, was a palpable mass of demons. Literally shivering as she sat down, I asked, "Mary, do you realize what followed you into my office?"

She fearfully nodded yes.

"Do you mind if I get rid of them?"

I'll never forget the shock on her face as she said, "You can *do* that?"

In a casual tone I commanded, "Okay, that's enough. Get out, all of you, now."

It felt as if the tide rolled out as the demonic mass left the room. No longer shivering, Mary was peaceful and quite surprised at the difference.

I said, "That was good . . . wasn't it?" She nodded in agreement.

"Would you like to see something better than that?" She nodded again.

"Holy Spirit," I prayed, "I invite you to come and rest upon Mary right now." And as quickly as the spirits had left, God wrapped her in His warm embrace. Again she was amazed, tears now streaming down her face.

"Mary, God's Spirit is resting on you; and the good news is, you can have His Spirit living *in* you. But before we talk about that, do you know what your god calls my God?"

She shook her head no.

"Then read this for me." I handed her Isaiah 14:14, and she read, "I will make myself *like the Most High*."

"Now, why would you worship a wannabe god, when you can worship the true and living God?" That day Mary chose to worship the true God.

* * *

Satan has marshaled his forces to help him ascend in power and to prevent God from being worshiped. He seeks to steal and wreck everything and everyone he touches. He's no novice; for thousands of years he has perfected his deception.

Illustrating well-designed trickery, Chuck Swindoll once said,

> A friend of mine ate dog food one evening. No, he wasn't at a fraternity initiation or a hobo party . . . he was actually at an elegant student reception in a physician's home near Miami. The dog food was served on delicate little crackers with a wedge of imported cheese, bacon chips, an olive, and a sliver of pimento on top. That's right, friends and neighbors—it was hors d'oeuvres *a la Alpo.*
>
> The hostess is a first-class nut! You gotta know her to appreciate the story. She had just graduated from a gourmet cooking course, and so she decided it was time to put her skill to the ultimate test. Did she ever! After doctoring up those

miserable morsels and putting them on a couple of silver trays, with a sly grin she watched them disappear. One guy (my friend) couldn't get enough. He kept coming back for more. I don't recall how they broke the news to him . . . but when he found out the truth, he probably barked and bit her on the leg! He certainly must have gagged a little.[1]

That's funny. The devil's traps are not.

As Jesus called Simon Peter and his brother Andrew from their fishing nets to follow Him, He said, "I will make you fishers of men" (Matthew 4:19). To be certain, *Satan likewise fishes for people*, baiting men and women away from God. Like many others before her, he had reeled Mary, the young lady in my office, into worshiping him. His bait? A lure. A lure is made to look like a real minnow, or frog, or worm, or whatever. But it isn't. It's a trick, and it's filled with hooks and barbs.

Today Satan is luring men, women, boys, girls, leaders, and followers to bow before him. His goal is to own the world, and he's not going to release his rule easily. It must be taken from him, and we must be a generation who will do it. Never forget, he is ruthless. To him, all's fair in love and war.

INSIGHTS TO REMEMBER

- God created man (male and female) and gave them dominion over the earth.
- Satan infiltrated the garden, challenged God's integrity, accused God to Eve, deceived Eve, and she and Adam gave earthly dominion over to him.
- Just as Satan tempted Eve, thousands of years later he tempted Christ in the wilderness, offering Him the nations.

- Adam and Eve gave earthly rule to Satan; spiritual warfare is a reversal of that transaction.

- Satan has marshaled his forces to help him ascend and to prevent God from being worshiped.

- Satan fishes for people, luring them to bow down to him.

- Satan won't release rule easily.

CHAPTER 5

THE GROUND-LEVEL BATTLEFIELD

There are three levels on which we may encounter the enemy: the ground level, the occult level, and the strategic (or territorial) level. I'll lend a chapter to each.

We call the first level "ground" because it's conducted right here on good ol' *terra firma*. In this realm, demons seek to affect, attach themselves to, or inhabit individuals. Here warfare involves confrontations with our Adamic nature, with temptations and torments that come our way from the world's system, and with altercations with evil spirits. Whether or not we're discerning enough to recognize them, all of these are common to life here.

Charles, a dedicated, relatively new Christian, came to me for counsel one day. "Pastor Eddie," he said sadly, "I think I may have a demon."

"Why is that?" I asked.

"It seems that no matter how disinterested I try to be, when I see a beautiful, scantily clad woman, I'm tempted to lust."

I said, "Charles, when your mind reaches out to lust after her, do you allow it, or do you 'slap its hand'?"

"Oh, Pastor, I slap its hand."

"That's good, because lust, when left unchecked, will conceive and give birth to sin. Here, though, you're dealing with your lower nature—your flesh—rather than a demon." (See James 1:15.)

I reminded him that being confronted with nudity, when you have no other option, isn't sin. Else there would be no Christian doctors and even fewer missionaries! King David's sin wasn't "seeing" Bathsheba bathing on her rooftop. He looked, lingered, and lusted; his lust gave birth to sin (see 2 Samuel 11).

Like many new believers, Charles had assumed that being saved meant an end to temptation. Not so. *Being saved means becoming equipped to overcome temptation rather than always being overcome by it* (see 1 Corinthians 10:13).

Jesus taught us to pray daily for a restraining order against Satan: "Deliver us from the evil one" (Matthew 6:13). This is, of course, one aspect of warfare prayer. However, beyond and in addition to our own spiritual self-defense, we are to defend one another. Intercessory prayer is praying for other people, places, and causes. Through intercession we partner with God in extending His kingdom.

DELIVERANCE MINISTRY

Another ground-level assignment is for personal (individual) deliverance from the power of the enemy. This is the process of freeing ourselves and others who are held captive in one or more areas of life. And it's more than prayer for protection. This is direct, hand-to-hand combat with spirits of darkness in what is commonly called "deliverance ministry."[1]

Deliverance ministry involves *casting out* and *crowding out* demons, as Jesus did and as He taught His followers (including us) to do. We call the casting-out process a *power encounter*, and we call the crowding-out process a *truth encounter*. In most instances, effective deliverance involves a measure of both.

Because we live on this ground level, spending all our days and nights here, this primarily is where we will confront our *three* enemies:

- our flesh (our fallen, lower nature);
- the world system (which languishes under the curse of sin);
- the devil (Satan).

The apostle Paul highlights the impact of these enemies as descriptive of us before we received Christ:

> You were dead in your transgressions and sins, in which you used to live when you followed *the ways of this world* and of *the ruler of the kingdom of the air*, the spirit who is now at work in those who are disobedient. All of us also lived among them at one time, gratifying the cravings of *our sinful nature* and following its desires and thoughts. Like the rest, we were by nature objects of wrath. (Ephesians 2:1–3, emphasis mine)

We were lost, and, to one degree or another, we were in league with or even helplessly dominated by Satan.

The Flesh

At the moment of salvation (justification), we who had sinned and fallen short of God's glory received (1) the divine nature of Christ and (2) a supernatural capacity to bring Him glory (see Romans 3:23; 1 John 5:12; Colossians 1:27).

For now, though, we also have retained our Adamic nature—the lower nature, the one that's fallen, the one that's sometimes referred to as "the flesh." *Flesh* doesn't refer to our physical bodies, in this case, but rather to our fallen sinful nature. We call this condition—having Christ's nature *and* still having our old nature—the "dual nature" of man.

John, in 1 John 2:16 (see KJV), explains that the world appeals to our sinful nature through the lust of the flesh (sinful cravings), the lust of the eyes (more than mere sexual desire), and the pride of life (insistence on "me first"). This is what Charles was learning about his new life. He still had an *inside* enemy to be addressed—his own nature.

* * *

By analogy, consider Israel's journey out of bondage toward freedom. When God gave them the Promised Land, it still was replete with formidable foes. They had many, many battles to fight there in order to possess and inhabit their land. God left the enemies in place so they could learn to fight and conquer. The same is true with us.

The divine nature we receive from the Lord, when properly embraced and applied, gives us power over our lower nature and its tendencies to sin. Nevertheless, this is a daily, moment-by-moment challenge for us to undertake, in obedience and humility, as God establishes His kingdom rule (the lordship of Christ) in us.

Until we've effectively learned to conquer our fallen nature and its lusts, we will continue to be obstructed and frustrated regarding our warfare. (I cover the issues pertaining to personal deliverance and victorious living more thoroughly in my book *Breaking the Enemy's Grip*.)[2]

The World

We will also face challenges from this world's system. We are continually bombarded with worldly temptation against which we must stand faithfully. Personal relationships, amusements, and entertainment aligned with darkness exert constant pressure on us. Unfortunately, our lower nature is naturally susceptible to this world's allurement.

> Be strong in the Lord and in his mighty power. Put on the full armor of God so that you can take your stand against the devil's schemes. For our struggle is not against flesh and blood, but against the rulers, against the authorities, against the powers of this dark world and against the spiritual forces of evil in the heavenly realms. Therefore *put on the full armor of God, so that when the day of evil comes, you may be able to stand your ground, and after you have done everything, to stand.* (Ephesians 6:10–13, emphasis mine)

The Devil

Finally, we can expect spirits of darkness to confront us with accusations, lies, enticements, and other strategies of wickedness. Demons, taking advantage of the world system, in cooperation with our old fleshly nature, will always challenge us to abort God's plan and yield to sin. Our warfare success in this arena is absolutely vital.

Jesus authorized His disciples, and each of us, to cast out demons (see Matthew 10:1–3; cf. Luke 10). If you want to learn even more about deliverance ministry, Alice's book *Delivering the Captives* is an excellent place to start.[3]

OPEN DOORS TO DARKNESS

How do Satan and his emissaries establish their rule in an individual's life? Evil's ground-level victories are a result of one or more of these factors.

Unholy Associations

We have ministered deliverance to many people who became demonized through their associations with others. The association can be anything from fornication to adultery to cult activity to occult practices (see chapter 6). The impartation of demons, as well as the Holy Spirit's anointing, can be conducted through the laying on of hands. This is especially true in the case of cults, which directly invite satanic involvement in their twisting and distortion of the truth. This is one reason thoughtful pastors do not allow anyone they don't know or haven't trained to minister at the altar during their services.

Generational Iniquity

Some people "inherit" demonic bondage as transmitted through the iniquity of their parents and grandparents. They bear no guilt for—that is, they carry no responsibility for—the sins of their fore-bears; however, when, for instance, a man is a womanizer, and as a result he attracts demonic spirits of sexual immorality, those spirits will inevitably affect his offspring. His children and their children will be left to deal with similar temptations with weaknesses and tendencies they've inherited from him. Through sin, he has left the door open to the enemy, and *that door remains open until someone closes it.*

God is a multi-generational God (Exodus 20:4–6; Numbers 14:17–19; Deuteronomy 5:8–10; 7:9; cf. Genesis 50:24; Exodus 3:6, 15–16). And never forget, Satan, without the ability to create, mimics God. The devil moves through generations to accomplish his goals as well.

In my book *Breaking the Enemy's Grip,* I explain how to break generational iniquity off of your life. You need not continue a wicked tendency because of the family into which you were born. You can, and you should, initiate and establish new, righteous generational tendencies.

Trauma

Some people (especially children) become demonized as a result of trauma. I'm reminded of one middle-aged woman who'd been plagued all her life by demons. One night, while we were praying for her at the church altar, a demonic manifestation occurred. When I asked the spirit its name, it answered, "Burn." (Odd name, isn't it?)

When I asked the woman if she'd ever been significantly burned, she explained how she'd been saved from a house fire when she was two. She hadn't been burned in the fire—it was her fear, or her trauma, that opened the door and gave the demons access. Imagine the terror of a two-year-old in a blazing building. Evil spirits took advantage of that moment.

That night she finally was set free from a demon who for decades had taken advantage of her childhood traumatic experience.

Later the same night she called her elderly mother to describe her newfound freedom; her mother then acknowledged that she had been praying for her daughter's deliverance all these years. She wanted to live long enough to see her daughter set free. Within a short time her mother went to be with Jesus—having rejoiced to see her number-one prayer answered!

Willful Sin

Demonization is most frequently a result of personal sin. When we sin, we yield ourselves to the kingdom of darkness; we obey Satan rather than God (see Romans 1; 1 John 5:16). Satan is a legal expert (see Ephesians 4:26-27), and his demons stand officiously upon "the contracts" we make with them (see Ephesians 2:1–3).

Are there sins one can commit that more quickly or completely "open the door" to the demonic? It seems that there are, and three come to mind.

The first is same-sex sin. Perhaps this is the case because God created man as man and woman as woman. Neither homosexuality nor lesbianism is a true sexual identity. They are avenues of perversion, the practice of which insults God and defies the natural creative order that flows from His very essence. In ministry, we've noticed that a single same-sex encounter often results in demonization.

The second sin that more quickly and completely opens the door to demons is cult or occult practice (e.g., see Acts 19:18–19). This includes involvement with elements like Satanism, witchcraft, New Age practices, shamanism, esoteric philosophies (such as Tibetan

Buddhism), humanism, certain music or movies, blood sacrifices, and consulting mediums or an Ouija board. These sins facilitate and perpetrate demonization because the practitioners have *personally* and *directly* solicited satanic power. We'll cover this more in the next chapter.

Third, while perhaps you can't imagine yourself ever being involved with the occult or giving yourself over to a cult, how about resentment and bitterness? Do you forgive easily? Are you harboring unforgiveness in your heart toward anyone living or dead? Jesus himself warns us that if we refuse to forgive others, God the Father will release us to "the tormentors" (Matthew 18:34 KJV).

* * *

So when we sin, we submit ourselves to serve evil. The more we commit a specific sin, the more habitual it becomes. The more habitual it becomes, the more we attract demonic spirits of that nature toward us and around us. Since it is sin that gives the enemy his authority—his only authority—demons look for people who are like themselves.

For example, a demon of fear isn't a spirit that provokes a person to be afraid. A demon of fear is a demon that *is* afraid. As the adage suggests, "birds of a feather flock together"; a fearful person attracts spirits of fear. The spirit of fear waits for the time when that person submits and buys into fear to the point that the spirit gains "legal right" to attach itself to or even enter that person. Now the once-fearful person has become *supernaturally* fearful.

Likewise, lying spirits are looking for liars. When they find a deceiver, it's as if they follow and lie in wait for him or her to cross an unseen line that effectively gives them legal right to attach to or inhabit the person. From the moment of demonization, the victim is no longer simply a liar; the lying spirits that inhabit him now empower him to the point that he is a "super liar." He has moved from liar to habitual liar to pathological liar.

You may be asking, Where is this "unseen line," and how can I know if I've crossed it? Truth is, no one knows exactly. However, if a person continues to excuse his sin rather than repent of it, his sin will become habitual, and he will ultimately build into his own life a demonic stronghold that at some point unknown to us *will* be inhabited by demonic spirits. Sin is serious.

CAN A CHRISTIAN HAVE A DEMON?

One concept that may make the answer to this question easier for us to comprehend is to know where demons reside in a person. For one thing, the word usually translated *possessed* is better rendered as *demonized*. When we say a person is demon possessed, this is what we mean—that they are being affected by or harassed by or overpowered by demons.

Demons are spirit beings that aren't limited by time and space. However, they dwell on the earth (see Job 1:7); in the atmosphere (see Ephesians 2:2; Jude 6); in items (see Exodus 7:11–12; Acts 19:19); in animals (see Genesis 3:1; Mark 5:12); and in people, including men (see Mark 1:23), women (see Luke 8:2), girls (see Mark 7:25), and boys (see Mark 9:17).

When they are "in" a person, demons attach themselves to the body and/or the soul—mind, will, and emotions. The Holy Spirit, on the other hand, lives within the person's spirit.

Can a Christian have a demon? My answer: A Christian can have anything he or she wants.

* * *

Do you remember Jesus' encounter with the Phoenician woman? She came to Him and pleaded, "Lord, have mercy on me. My daughter is suffering from demon possession." After listening to her begging, Jesus answered, "I was sent to the lost sheep of Israel." Her reply again was, "Lord, help me" (see Mark 7:24–30; here, my paraphrase). He replied, "It is not right to take the children's bread and toss it to their dogs" (v. 27).

Jesus was saying that deliverance was for the children. *We* are God's children, grafted into the household of faith. Jesus showed the disciples that deliverance shouldn't be attempted with lost people unless salvation follows, lest the house be left clean—but empty (see Matthew 12:29, 44–45).

A good example is something that happened to me back in the early 1970s. I was new to deliverance work and didn't yet understand many of its principles. One night there was a tormented teenage girl to whom Alice and I ministered. Naïvely, we carefully cast the demons out of her, but shock and sadness soon overruled our temporary joy.

She was found dead two days later at the bottom of a friend's swimming pool. Honestly, I had never checked to see whether or not she was born again. I fervently focused on the enemy and ignored the issue of her relationship with Christ. With good intentions I helped free her from her demons, but then I left her house "clean but empty." The enemy, whose goal, once again, is to steal, kill, and destroy, returned to find the empty house and set about to violently reclaim it.

The English word *deliverance* comes from a Greek term that's also translated *salvation*. Deliverance from demons is nothing more than the continuation of our salvation (sanctification). In some cases, deliverance precedes the moment of salvation (justification). In others, salvation precedes deliverance.

DELIVERANCE GUIDELINES

Now let's consider some of what is needed in deliverance ministry.

(1) Diagnosis doesn't necessarily mean assignment.

Knowing that someone might need deliverance doesn't necessarily constitute your marching orders to do anything other than pray.

- A demonized person typically has one or more areas of his life out of control.
- Pray for the Lord to open the doors for his deliverance.
- Fast for his freedom.
- Pray for the enemy to be exposed and defeated in his life.
- Wait for the Holy Spirit. If you discover that you are the one assigned to bring freedom to him, he will be drawn to you. One day, out of the blue, he may say something like, "You know, I feel God wants to use you to help me." When God has prepared the way, victory is assured!

(2) Authority supersedes anointing.

In every spiritual structure there is also an authority structure. If you can't submit to authority (regardless of your anointing), then God can't afford to extend your boundaries. Joseph had an anointing to interpret dreams. He spoke prophetically to his brothers and, years later, to his fellow prisoners. Nevertheless, at that time he had no authority. God tested Joseph, allowing authority to rule over and even mistreat him. Once Joseph was proven to understand and carry real authority with a right attitude, the Lord changed his situation. He will do the same for you in whatever way is according to His plan.

(3) Struggles for power and control breed premature responsibility.

Alice had a situation some years back when she was visiting a church with a friend. The pastor knew of her ministry of deliverance, but when at the altar he began to wrestle with demons in a woman, he never called on Alice to assist. Later she told me that the burden to set this woman free was burning in her heart, but she respected the authority of the church. It would have been inappropriate for her to rush to the altar and intervene or take over. The authority you learn to appreciate will be the authority given to you in time.

Why? Oswald Chambers might have said it best in *My Utmost for His Highest*: "When His life has been created in me by His redemption, I instantly recognize His right to absolute authority over me."[4]

Once we fully grasp God's absolute reign in our lives, and we then bend to His calling through acts of obedience, complete surrender will have begun to find a serious and secure home in us.

A person who's still fighting Christ's lordship and giving in to the flesh isn't ready to cast out devils. Have you been given authority by Jesus? Yes. Have you gained authority through prayer and intimacy with God? This requires time and testing. And wisdom.

(4) Credibility opens doors.

Exercise spiritual discernment when casting out demons.

- Don't abuse the person to whom you're ministering.
- Always respect the dignity of others.

- Don't be foolish; don't exhibit bizarre behavior, wild actions, or unreasonable demands.

- Don't be intimidated by demons.

- Honor the guidelines that are given you.

- Realize that not all problems can be solved in one session.

- While sometimes deliverance occurs instantly, it's often progressive.

- Don't be a know-it-all. Remain humble and teachable.

- Ask the Lord to help you stay in balance.

- Don't confess aloud your lack of knowledge or fear to do deliverance. (Demons can't read your mind; you give them information when you speak.)

THE PURPOSE OF DELIVERANCE MINISTRY

When asked, "What is the purpose of deliverance ministry?" most everyone answers, "freedom." Actually, the ultimate purpose of deliverance ministry is the same as the purpose for everything we do: *the glory of God* (see 1 Corinthians 10:31). Unless we understand this, we'll be off track in the process.

In some cases, deliverance would result in freedom but not bring glory to God. Some people want to be free from demonic oppression, obsession, or "possession" so they can be free to live the way *they* please, rather than loving and serving the Lord with their freedom. You may remember that the apostle Paul was tormented by "a messenger of Satan." Three times he prayed to God to remove the torment and set him free. And three times God said no.

Later Paul understood why. The "thorn in [his] flesh" remained so that he wouldn't become prideful (see 2 Corinthians 12:6–8). In this instance, God's highest goal was not Paul's personal freedom but that He might receive glory through his life. Paul spent most of his Christian life in prison. He brought glory to God in chains and suffering!

As we win ground-level battles against sin, we are being equipped to move into the next level of warfare. Remember: The air war can't be effectively waged unless and until we've addressed the battles inside us, and the battles with others.

INSIGHTS TO REMEMBER

- Being saved doesn't mean freedom from temptation; it means becoming equipped for victory over it.

- Deliverance ministry is the process of freeing ourselves and others who are being acted upon by demons.

- The English word *deliverance* comes from a Greek word that's also translated *salvation*. Deliverance is part of the process of our salvation.

- Our three enemies are our flesh (fallen, lower nature), the world's system (which languishes under the curse of sin), and the devil.

- At the moment of salvation (justification), we receive the divine nature of Christ.

- Demons enter a person as a result of personal sin, ungodly associations, generational iniquity, and/or trauma.

- When we sin, we submit ourselves to serve Satan.

- Sin that's repeated becomes habitual. (Habitual sin builds a stronghold [a house of thoughts contrary to the Word of God] that at some point can become inhabited by a strongman [prince demon].)

- Demons typically reside in the body or the soulish areas (mind, will, and emotions) of a person.

- Deliverance sometimes occurs instantly, but it's often progressive, with acts of repentance and obedience.

- Diagnosis doesn't necessarily mean assignment.

- The authority you learn to appreciate will be the authority given to you in time.

- Deliverance requires discernment and calls for great humility.

- The purpose of deliverance is the same as the purpose for everything—the glory of God!

CHAPTER 6

THE OCCULT-LEVEL BATTLEFIELD

"Pastor Eddie," invoked the church secretary over the office intercom. "The principal of the high school would like to speak with you." I picked up the phone, greeted the principal, and asked her how I could help.

She told me how she and school security officers were discovering that more and more of their students were turning to the occult. Some, she suspected, were doing so out of curiosity. Others were being led by fellow students. And still others seemed deeply involved in witchcraft, Satanism, and the like. "I've heard about you and your wife and your ministry," she said. "Do you have any idea why a substantial number of our kids would be moving in this direction?"

"Have you attended church lately?" I asked.

"Yes, indeed. We rarely miss a service," she replied.

"Have you seen the power of God demonstrated in your services?"

"Well, uh . . . not really."

"*That's* why. Your students are looking for demonstrations of spiritual power. (See 1 Corinthians 4:20.) When few are seeing it in their churches, many naturally will look into the occult." Young people naturally look for spiritual power.

* * *

The occult level of spiritual warfare is where people solicit demons for spiritual power. The truth? Pretending to accept a partnership, the demons immediately plan their solicitors' destruction.

At the onset, these demons willingly capitulate to human manipulation to gain greater control later. Even a young child, knowing the procedures, can persuade demons to perform; and perform they will, like trick ponies, *until they gain more and more control*. Then the demons begin to manipulate, break down, and ultimately destroy the human who sought their power. Deception and betrayal are their tools.

DEEPER AND DEEPER INTO FALSEHOOD

In the 1990s, during Operation Desert Storm, after Iraq had invaded tiny Kuwait, the entire world impatiently held its collective breath awaiting the U.S.-led Allied ground forces' assault on Iraqi military positions. Perhaps because we Texans are known to enjoy a fight, many of us thought the ground war would *never* begin. But General Norman Schwarzkopf had a plan . . . a strategy. The ground war would not begin until the air war was completed.

Sure enough, just as he had promised, once the air war was finished, the ground war began—if you could call it a war. Saddam Hussein's soldiers were disillusioned, their communication system was devastated, and their military strength dissipated. Most surrendered peacefully on the spot. In many ways, despite the desert heat, the ground war was as predicted: "no sweat."

By contrast, *we* are not fighting a flesh-and-blood war. Our battles are against forces of darkness, and the rules of engagement appear to be just the opposite. *In our conflict, the air war cannot begin until the ground war is completed.*

We've discussed the necessity of our winning the ground war; now we'll turn our attention to the air war. The second warfare level is the occult battlefield.

Occult-level spiritual warfare refers to our intercessory confrontations with demonic forces that operate through Satanism, witchcraft, New Age practices, shamanism, false religions, secular humanism, media that glorifies the occult, blood sacrifices, and so on. This level of warfare—fighting with our feet off the ground, so to speak—tends to be tougher for two reasons.

First, although some victims (especially the young) have been seduced and trapped by subtle demonic deception, many others have openly, willfully solicited satanic power.

Second, the very nature of occult involvement is about seeking other "gods" and/or endeavoring to become as God. Even worse is lusting to possess "godlike power" and giving oneself over to manipulating persons, situations, and objects. Whether it is out of a desire to manipulate for good or for bad, all of this is at the heart of witchcraft. We are to have no other gods before Jehovah (see Exodus 20). *God reserves lordship for himself.*

New Age religions, in all of their facets, are empowered by

occult-level spirits. These are the belief systems promoted by Rhonda Byrne (author of *The Secret*), by Oprah Winfrey, and by many others. Foundationally, the basis of this worldview is that you and I are our own gods, and we need look no further than within ourselves.

It's foolish enough to believe what is straightaway false. It's even more damaging to blend falsehoods with truth. It's tragic that many actually consider there to be a "Church of Oprah," because the Oprahfication of Christianity is blindness-inducing and blasphemous.

Recently Oprah was asked, "How were you able to reconcile these spiritual teachings with your Christian beliefs?" This was her response.

> I was able to open my mind about the absolute, indescribable hugeness of that which we call "God."
>
> I took God out of the box, because I grew up in the Baptist church and there were rules, and belief systems, and doctrines.
>
> I happened to be sitting in church in my late twenties. And I was going to this church where you had to get there at eight o'clock in the morning or you couldn't get a seat . . . a very charismatic minister . . . and everybody was into the sermon. And this great minister was preaching about how great God was, and how omniscient, and omnipresent and "God is everything." Then he said, *"The Lord thy God is a jealous God."*[1]
>
> And I was caught up in the rapture of that moment until he said "jealous," and something struck me. I was about twenty-seven or twenty-eight [years old], thinking *God is all, God is omnipresent, and God is also* jealous? *God is jealous of* me?[2] Something about that didn't feel right in my spirit, because I believed that God is love and that God is in all things.

So that's when the search for something more than doctrine started to stir within me. And I love this quote that Eckhart [Tolle] has, one of my favorite quotes in chapter one [of his book *A New Earth: Awakening to Your Life's Purpose*], where he says, "Man made God in his own image. The eternal, infinite, and unnamable was reduced to a mental idol that you had to believe in and worship as 'my God' or 'our God.'" And I think that's very eloquently put by Eckhart. . . .

That is exactly what I was feeling when I was sitting in church that Sunday listening to the preacher. And it's been a journey to get to the place where I understand . . . that what I believe is that Jesus came to show us "Christ consciousness." Jesus came to show us "the way of the heart," and that what Jesus was saying [is that he will] show us the "higher consciousness". . . . Jesus came to say, "Look, I'm going to live in the body, in the human body, and I'm gonna show you how it's done. These are some principles and some laws that you can use to live by, to know that 'way.'" And when I started to recognize that, that Jesus didn't come—in my belief, even as a Christian—I don't believe that Jesus came to start Christianity. So that was also very comforting. . . .

There's a wonderful book called *Discover the Power Within You* by Eric Butterworth, which helps me reconcile the two. So that might be really good for those of you who are Christians. . . . [3]

That's what Oprah had to say about Jesus Christ. Let's consider what He has to say about those who would deny His teaching.

[When] we all reach unity in the faith and in the knowledge of the Son of God and become mature, attaining to the whole measure of the fullness of Christ[,] then we will no longer be infants, tossed back and forth by the waves, and blown here and there by every wind of teaching and by the cunning and craftiness of men in their deceitful scheming. Instead, speaking the truth in love, we will in all things grow up into him who is the Head, that is, Christ. (Ephesians 4:13–15)

The time will come when [people] will not put up with sound doctrine. Instead, to suit their own desires, they will gather around them a great number of teachers to say what their itching ears want to hear. They will turn their ears away from the truth and turn aside to myths. (2 Timothy 4:3–4)

You must teach what is in accord with sound doctrine. (Titus 2:1)

Anyone who runs ahead and does not continue in the teaching of Christ does not have God; whoever continues in the teaching has both the Father and the Son. If anyone comes to you and does not bring this teaching, do not take him into your house or welcome him. (2 John 9–10)

In *Breaking Strongholds in Your City,* compiled and edited by C. Peter Wagner, Cindy Jacobs writes:

I see occultic strongholds as an overt evil application of many ideological strongholds. Occultic strongholds are strongholds of witchcraft, Satanism and New Age religions, which invite spirit guides to operate. They work as "power boosters" to the territorial spirits that dwell over geographic regions.

The territorial spirits over a city or region are greatly empowered by the occult spells, curses, rituals and fetishes used by witches, warlocks and Satanists. Ruling powers of darkness manipulate those involved in the occult to do their bidding and attempt to destroy the power of the church and the reign of God in an area. Christian leaders are often unaware that this is really happening in their city. Many pastors and leaders are themselves under tremendous satanic attack and either they do not realize what is going on or they are so beat-up, discouraged and weary that they cannot fight the onslaught. This is not something we need to fear, but we do need to understand and fight against the wiles or methods of the enemy.

One of the ways [occultists] assault Christians and leaders is by sending curses. This is done through spells, unholy intercession and fastings. Ezekiel 13:18 says, "Woe to the women who sew magic charms on their sleeves and make veils for the heads of people of every height to hunt souls!"[4]

CULTS AND THE OCCULT: HOW MUCH DO WE *REALLY* NEED TO KNOW?

Ever since I wrote *Breaking the Enemy's Grip* (and, ever since Alice and I wrote *Spiritual Housecleaning*),[5] people continually come to me with video games, New Age materials, movies, and the like, asking if I will "check things out for them." I rarely do. Why?

First, any list I could compile would be obsolete in a week. Evil, like a chameleon, continually changes colors and forms in order to deceive. In our world there are tens of thousands of false religions and cults. While many people are devoted to ancient religions, others are devoted to religions that didn't exist six months ago.

Second, you need not depend upon my list. The Holy Spirit, who lives in you, has been given to guide you into all truth. You must learn to rely on Him and on the Scriptures.

Third, on the whole, such things don't merit having attention drawn to them: "Have nothing to do with the barren unprofitable deeds of darkness, but, instead of that, set your faces against them; for the things which are done by these people in secret it is disgraceful even to speak of" (Ephesians 5:11–12, WNT).

There will be times in your walk with God when you must draw aside and pay attention to evil that's affecting your life and your home. Nevertheless, that will be temporary, primarily to purify yourself or to prepare for warfare prayer. Otherwise, Christ alone should be your focus! "I desire you to be truly wise as to good, but simple toward evil" (Romans 16:19 LITV).

To be sure, some Christians are called of God to study these things, but they do so with His direction and according to His will.

And fourth, I'm not going to do your research for you. If you want to know more about an issue, all you need is a computer with online access. If you don't have one, go to your local public library. Start using a search engine (like Google), and you'll quickly find more information than you can imagine.[6]

HOW TO IDENTIFY A CULT

First, a cult is an individual or group that recommends or requires you to bow your knee to anyone or anything other than the Lord Jesus Christ. "There's one God and only one" (1 Timothy 2:5 THE MESSAGE).

Second, a cult is an individual or group that proposes any other way to God than through Jesus Christ (see John 14:6).

Third, a cult is an individual or group that suggests any other solution for your sin than the blood of Jesus. "There's . . . one Priest-Mediator between God and us—Jesus, who offered himself in exchange for everyone held captive by sin, to set them all free" (1 Timothy 2:5–6 THE MESSAGE).

Fourth, a cult is an individual or group that proposes that your eternal salvation is provided in any other way than through the death, burial, and resurrection of Christ (see John 11:25).

Fifth, a cult is an individual or group that recommends that you add anything (any work of your own) to Christ's death, burial, and resurrection in order to be saved (see 2 Corinthians 11:4).

Sixth, a cult is an individual or group that offers you spiritual rules or regulations other than those God clearly teaches.

> The Spirit makes it clear that as time goes on, some are going to give up on the faith and chase after demonic illusions put forth by professional liars. These liars have lied so well and for so long that they've lost their capacity for truth. They will tell you not to get married. They'll tell you not to eat this or that food—perfectly good food God created to be eaten heartily and with thanksgiving by believers who know better! Everything God created is good, and to be received with thanks. Nothing is to be sneered at and thrown out. God's Word and our prayers make every item in creation holy.
>
> You've been raised on the Message of the faith and have followed sound teaching. Now pass on this counsel to the followers of Jesus there, and you'll be a good servant of Jesus.
> (1 Timothy 4:1–6 THE MESSAGE)

Seventh, a cult is an individual or group with any philosophy or activity that refers to accessing or relying on forces, spirits, powers, energies, etc., other than the Holy Spirit. Or anything that offers you spiritual enlightenment (apart from God's Word). God's Word is a lamp to your feet and a light for your path (see Psalm 119:105).

Example: On a Web site promoting occult healing, I find:

> Reiki is one of the few healing modalities that is used for self-healing and for the healing of others. In Reiki, students receive *"attunements,"* which *empower* them to do Reiki.

The attunement is a *spiritual process* where *healing energy* is *activated* and *enhanced*.

In that one sentence I have italicized six terms that should be red flags to anyone seeking the truth.

And eighth, a cult is an individual or group who insists on absolute loyalty to a person or a group. True men and women of God will insist that you trust God alone and totally commit yourself to the lordship of Jesus Christ.[7]

THE IMPORTANCE OF PATIENCE AND HUMILITY

Many prophetically gifted people can almost *taste* the air war; lots of intercessors are ready and willing to lead the charge in the heavenlies. They've been dreaming of the day and revving up their engines for years. They're on the edge of their seats, waiting until the Lord releases them against hell's gates. Like many during Desert Storm, some of these warriors are wondering, *Why not now? Let's get on with it!*

Others, overcome with impatience, have decided presumptuously to fight their own battles, determine their own targets, and call their own shots. They've moved out on their own, often with little or no directive from their Commander, the Lord of Hosts. They've conducted their own spiritual sorties (air raids) and have precious little to show for it. Many have suffered backlash, some are sick, and some have even died.

For instance, a few years ago, when Alice and I were ministering in Ecuador, one pastor approached me in obvious distress. He told me about a promising young woman who was becoming well-known as a pop singer, when she was born again and joined his church. He was thrilled!

He said,

> The Wednesday night prayer meetings at our church drew large crowds, among them this young girl—a new convert. For several months she watched and emulated one of our seasoned intercessors conduct a direct frontal assault against evil spirits.
>
> Some nights I wasn't involved, but when I heard her do this for the first time, I got chills of concern. As her pastor, I had the obligation to warn her, a new Christian, that it wasn't healthy for her to taunt and harass demons, especially those pertaining to witches in the area. [In South America, witches carry a powerful presence.] Pastor Eddie, I failed her, and I feel so guilty.
>
> One Wednesday night about a month ago she stood up and began to pace back and forth, ranting and raving, taunting demons. I cringed. Moments later, in midsentence, she dropped dead, instantly. We tried to revive her. The emergency care came. No change. The medical examiner was never able to determine the cause of death. But we know you can tell us, so would you please?

I consoled the weeping pastor, and then I carefully explained that the young lady was a baby Christian who had neither gained the right nor been given the authority to do what she was doing. I showed him how the authority Jesus grants us is *ambassadorial* in nature—to be used with His permission and under His direction. The girl had been defeated by regional occult powers that had ruled the land for ages. She was sincere, but she was sincerely wrong, because she was neither equipped for nor assigned to the perilous duty she was trying to carry out.

Satan is clever. Shaking your fist in the air and declaring open war on high-ranking demons could cost you everything. You need to know that whatever you're doing and saying carries God's authority and not yours.

SPIRITS OF THE OCCULT . . . AND BEYOND

In Acts 16:16–23, we see how Paul dealt with a young woman who had a spirit of divination (or fortune-telling). Read the passage carefully.

Once when we were going to the place of prayer, we were met by a slave girl who had a spirit by which she predicted the future. She earned a great deal of money for her owners by fortune-telling. This girl followed Paul and the rest of us, shouting, "These men are servants of the Most High God, who are telling you the way to be saved."

She kept this up for many days. Finally Paul became so troubled that he turned around and said to the spirit, "In the name of Jesus Christ I command you to come out of her!" At that moment the spirit left her.

When the owners of the slave girl realized that their hope of making money was gone, they seized Paul and Silas and dragged them into the marketplace to face the authorities. They brought them before the magistrates and said, "These men are Jews, and are throwing our city into an uproar by advocating customs unlawful for us Romans to accept or practice."

The crowd joined in the attack against Paul and Silas, and the magistrates ordered them to be stripped and beaten. After they had been severely flogged, they were thrown into prison, and the jailer was commanded to guard them carefully.

A spirit of divination (fortune-telling) was known in that day as a spirit of Python, or Apollo. According to mythology, Python, a huge serpent that lived on Mount Parnasus, was famous for predicting future events. Apollo, the Greek god of (among other things) prophecy, music, and light, slew this serpent and from then on also was called Pythias. He became a celebrated cultic symbol of the oracle; the belief, generally, was that "the spirit of Apollo Pythias" influenced all revealed things yet to come.

At any rate, Paul and Silas were going to pray, when the slave girl accosted and harassed them, and she did this repeatedly. It should come as no surprise to us that the enemy loves to distract saints from prayer.

Paul knew this girl had an evil spirit. But wasn't she telling the truth about them, saying they were servants of the Lord and telling others about salvation? Indeed, she *was* telling the truth. But we need to see beyond the obvious to understand Satan's purpose. The evil design, working through her, was to diminish the apostles' message by making people think they were in league with this demonized medium, thus influencing them to conclude that the source of Paul's and Silas' prophecies and miracles was the same as the girl's prophecies, thus discrediting the gospel.

Although Paul knew the girl was demonized, he didn't let the demons dictate to him how and when he should respond. He didn't do anything to stop her until God gave him both the compassion and the command to exercise spiritual authority in the matter. Listen: We may have a revelation about something, or even the spiritual authority or anointing to deal with it, but that doesn't necessarily mean we have permission to act. As we have said and will say again, *"Diagnosis is not assignment"* (cf. Luke 10:19).

We don't know why Paul waited several days to rebuke the spirit. I'm reminded of Jesus waiting until after the death of Lazarus before going to him. At any rate, though, here are some possible reasons Paul waited before moving against the spirit of fortune-telling in the girl.

For one thing, maybe Paul had wanted time to carefully consider the outcome. This spirit seems to have been one of the ruling principalities over Philippi rather than an occult-level demon; if this is correct, Paul could expect the whole city to be thrown into an uproar upon the girl's exorcism (see Acts 16:20–23).

At the same time, maybe Paul had just been waiting for permission from the Lord to cast out the spirit. Remember what Jesus said in John 5:19? "I tell you the truth, the Son can do nothing by himself; he can only do what he sees the Father doing."

Or Paul might have been holding off until he was sure that with the assignment there would be victory (see Acts 16:25–28). Most likely this was not an occult-level spirit; there is sufficient biblical detail to suggest that she embodied a territorial spirit with power over the city. Why do I believe this is true? We'll see it as we study the strategic level of spiritual warfare, in the next chapter.

* * *

Although occult-level spiritual warfare includes deliverance, it involves more than merely casting out demons. There's a difference between, on the one hand, removing a demon of fear from someone who's afraid of the dark and, on the other, separating demons from a witch who's spent years soliciting the kingdom of darkness for spiritual power. Any person or community or territory that has been dedicated to Satan and/or that corporately embraces the occult is dealing with a stronger intensity of darkness. If you're going to fight at this level, you'd better have gained the spiritual authority to do so.

A CLEAR VIEW OF SATAN'S INTENT

Thinking back to the devil's origin and purpose, *why* does Satan war against God? Satan wars against God because he has the audacity to think he can displace God on heaven's throne. See his declaration of defiance:

> What a comedown this, O Babylon!
> > Daystar! Son of Dawn!
> Flat on your face in the underworld mud,
> > you, famous for flattening nations!
> You said to yourself,
> > "*I'll climb to heaven.*
> *I'll set my throne*
> > *over the stars of God.*
> *I'll run the assembly of angels*
> > *that meets on sacred Mount Zaphon.*
> *I'll climb to the top of the clouds.*
> > *I'll take over as King of the Universe!*"
> > (Isaiah 14:12–14 THE MESSAGE, emphasis mine)

Note his five-point declaration.

(1) I will climb to heaven.

(2) I will set my throne over God's stars.

(3) I will rule all of heaven's angels.

(4) I will climb to the top of the clouds.

(5) I will be King of the Universe.

Every time I read this passage I picture Jack, from the 1997 movie *Titanic*, standing at the ship's pulpit, arched over the ocean, shouting, "I'm the king of the world!" Well, Satan has much higher ambitions: He wants to govern the universe. And obviously he suffers from "*I* trouble" ("*I* will . . . *I* will . . . *I* will . . .").

But the best Satan can do is to imitate his Creator. He can't create anything; he can only take what God has created and try to pervert it into something that glorifies him rather than God. And the influence of his attempts to accomplish his diabolical goal has darkened entire cultures on the earth.

* * *

In the summer of 2005, our eldest son, Robert, and I traveled to India. The day we were to depart for home we asked to visit the Temple of Kali in Calcutta, one of the nation's oldest and most revered Hindu temples.

There in the blazing midday June heat we stood at the altar and watched as one by one baby goats were led in, scrubbed with soap and water, and had their tiny horns painted. Then the priest would place their little heads into a forked stump and swiftly behead them with a sharp ceremonial sword. As their blood splashed onto the cobblestone floor, he would dip his fingers into the blood and wipe it on the worshipers' foreheads, for which they would pay him a temple tithe.

At that point he would hand the carcass through a hole in the wall to a waiting butcher who would sell it in the temple meat market. The goats were "sold" twice: first as a sacrifice, then again as food.

As I observed these gory proceedings, I began to converse in my heart with the Father.

"Lord, why do they do this?"

"Satan makes them do it," He explained. "He wants to be like me. Bloody sacrifices were originally my idea, you know."

"True enough," I said. "But you haven't required a bloody sacrifice from man since Calvary; why does Satan still require this?"

The Father gently said, "Satan requires these bloody sacrifices from them because *Satan has no son.*"

Satan can never be like the Most High. It's as if when Christ died, the Father announced, "Checkmate, game over." The devil had no answer to the Son's sacrificial death.

So the bleating of every baby goat that's slaughtered in heathen temples around the world today declares, "Satan is a loser. He has lost!"

* * *

During that same experience, Robert and I had hardly arrived at the slaughter pen when one of the priests, about my age, slipped to my side.

"Do you understand what you are seeing?" he asked.

"Yes," I replied.

Then immediately he disregarded my answer and began explaining to me why they were slaughtering the animals.

"Sir, I said I *do* understand what you're doing. It's obvious that your goddess, Kali, desires that you offer her bloody sacrifices."

"Yes," he said with a smile.

"Sir, that's the difference between your goddess and my God. My God doesn't demand this from His worshipers. To the contrary, *He* offered a bloody sacrifice for *us*—His only Son, Jesus Christ."

Until that moment, everything was okay. Then, at the mention of one name, all hell broke loose. When I said, "God offered His only Son, Jesus, as a sacrifice for our sin," the priest went ballistic. He got into my face and began trying to shout me down. The crowd of worshipers from the four corners of the temple began moving toward the sound. The rifle-toting guards began to move in closely as well.

Finally, I said, "Sir, the reason you can't listen to what I'm saying is that the words I speak are 'hitting your heart.'"

Suddenly he drew very quiet.

"People of the temple," I went on. "Kali is no god. Jehovah God created heaven and earth and offered up His own Son, Jesus, as a sacrifice for your sin." For four or five minutes the Lord allowed me to preach the gospel in this occultic temple before we left.

THREE WARFARE PRINCIPLES

Let's close by noting three elements that are sorely needed when fighting occult-level battles.

(1) *There is no true power in emotional fervor.* As we say, demons are not deaf. Certainly at times we may raise our voices to communicate effectively or underscore a point, but not to access additional strength. There are times when with one quiet word deliverance will be effected.

(2) *Always run to the battle, not from the battle.* For example, you should not become frightened to discover that witches have moved into your neighborhood or city. Exercise faith. Look and listen for God's orders concerning them. And always remember that His directives will not contradict anything He's commanded us in His Word.

(3) *Undue focus on the devil gives him pleasure.* Satan knows that you'll not likely worship him. So he typically lures you toward overvaluing yourself. If he can cause you to keep your eyes and mind on yourself, or your fears, God is robbed of your attention. This was the error of the young Ecuadorian woman.

For the devil's purposes, one step beyond obsessing over ourselves is focusing on him. We must show more wisdom than this. Don't become enamored with him and his demons. And don't elevate a minister who focuses attention on Satan. Even someone who's used in powerful deliverance ministry will keep his or her focus on Christ Jesus alone!

INSIGHTS TO REMEMBER

- The occult level of spiritual warfare is where people solicit demons for spiritual power.
- Pretending to accept a partnership, the demons immediately are planning their solicitors' destruction.
- Some victims (especially the young) have been seduced and trapped by subtle demonic deception; many others have openly, willfully solicited satanic power.
- The desire to manipulate for good or for bad is at the heart of witchcraft.
- One of the ways occultists assault Christians and leaders is by sending curses.
- Any person or community or territory that has been dedicated to Satan and/or that corporately embraces the occult is dealing with a stronger intensity of darkness.

- Satan wars against God because he has the audacity to think he can seize heaven's throne.

- There is no true power in emotional fervor.

- Undue focus on the devil gives him pleasure. This becomes a power struggle and the devil knows he will win.

CHAPTER 7

THE TERRITORIAL-LEVEL BATTLEFIELD

In the summer of 1990, I heard about an event that had taken place in our city the night before the previous Halloween. It was "Breakthrough Houston," a citywide convocation of churches to do strategic-level spiritual battle for Houston. Our church was beginning to extend its outward vision, and we pastors felt it would be good if we participated the next time around.

I made contact with the host pastor, the one who'd convened the event, to express our desire to be involved; however, I was sad and surprised when he said, "Oh, we're not planning to repeat it this year."

Not going to repeat it? I marveled. I'd heard so many positive comments.

When I asked why, he began to recall a litany of disasters pertaining to the pastors and churches who'd already taken part. One pastor, soon after that night, had lost his church. Another's son had committed suicide. Another's wife left him. And on and on it went, a trail of anguish and agony all attributed to their participation in Breakthrough Houston.

"What exactly did you do last year?" I inquired.

He explained that they first had worshiped for more than an hour. Actually I learned later—from Alice and her friend Eraina, who had attended—that it was mostly warfare music,[1] along the lines of *"We're gonna stomp all over the devil's face, rah rah rah."* (I made that up, but you get my point.) Then he said that one by one leaders had come to the microphone to pray and speak against Satan and his territorial demonic princes above the city, while almost ten thousand attendees joined in the fervor.

As he spoke it became clear to me why the enemy had retaliated so viciously. I was reminded of a time when, as a child, I threw a rock at a hornet's nest. It had seemed like such a good idea at first . . . but in the end, I was the victim, not the victor.

* * *

The pre-Halloween event apparently had done little more than anger the kingdom of darkness, which then had taken vengeance against the pastors and leaders. I returned to our church and reported the conversation to our staff. Then we prayed and determined a plan of action through which, hopefully, we could convince that pastor to repeat the event.

We went back to him and made suggestions for altering the program. "If you'll agree to these changes," we said, "we'll help you recruit pastors and churches to participate this year."

"What do you have in mind?" he asked.

"First, let's have at least an hour of pure, Christ-centered praise and worship. Next, let's have individual pastors come to the microphone, not to rant and rail against demonic princes, but to announce a known sin in the churches of our city, and to lead us all, as representatives of the city church, in prayers of repentance.

"Then, let's pray prayers of replacement. For example: If we've repented of our pride, we'll ask God to give us hearts of humility.

"After repentance and replacement, we'll share the Lord's Supper.

"Finally, each person will be given a prayer covenant and a corporate declaration to announce to principalities above the city. Around 8:45 PM, in unison, we'll read our covenant of unity and pray aloud. Then, authoritatively, we'll read our declaration to break the power of the enemy over the city of Houston. We'll conclude the evening with exuberant praise and celebration."

He liked it! And we agreed to work together.

* * *

I was asked to lead worship at the event. As my team was tuning up, and as people were filing into the auditorium, I had three unrelated individuals come to me with the same message. "Satanists/witches have infiltrated the crowd tonight. They've read about this event in the papers and have come here to war against what we're doing." The wording was different each time, but the thought was essentially the same.

As I began the service, I welcomed everyone. Then, to the surprise of many, I said, "I've been told there are people who have come to combat what we're about to do. I want you to know that we're delighted you're here. You are in the safest place in this city— surrounded by people who love you and want only the best for your life. Before we begin, we're going to take a moment to ask God to bless you." And I did.

Later a woman from our church told me that a rather oddly dressed woman had been seated beside her with a large bag at her feet. "While you were preparing the service, she took several strange items out of her bag and laid them in her lap. There was a clump of hair, a collection of feathers, a bronze cross . . . fetishes—that's what they were. She was carefully arranging them when you mentioned blessing the witches. At that moment, she swept them up into her arms and began to cram them back into her sack. And she never pulled them out again."

Later that night several pastors privately told me they'd learned from my prayer. As they explained it, the natural thing would have been to pray *against* the witches. Nevertheless, they realized and affirmed that Jesus taught us to pray *for* our enemies (see Matthew 5:44).

* * *

We didn't learn until the next day about the evening's most amazing occurrence. On page 28A of the *Houston Chronicle* was an article, "What Were Those Lights in the Sky?" that read:

It was the stuff of an unsolved Halloween mystery, but authorities agreed that the UFO sighted in northwest Harris County and southwest Montgomery County on Tuesday night probably resulted from a meteor shower. Still, area law enforcement agencies, as well as fire stations, had no choice but to take the reports that came in about 8:45 PM seriously.

To us, this was a confirmation in the heavenlies—a brilliant flash of light that neither NASA, nor law enforcement, nor the National Weather Service could explain.

We believe it was the clash of the kingdom of light against the kingdom of darkness as thousands of repentant believers made declaration in unison and in unity. From that night, crime in Houston began to decrease. In December 1994, the *Houston Post* reported that violent crime had dropped 29.2 percent since January 1992. By 1995, the *Houston Chronicle* reported crime had dropped an additional 31.9 percent to a record decrease of 51.1 percent!

This level was maintained for several years, despite Houston's record population increase. It wasn't until the influx of refugees from New Orleans after Hurricane Katrina that we saw regrowth in crime, and *that* in the very neighborhoods where the refugees were relocated. (We were celebrated for receiving refugees and providing for their support. However, we failed to maintain our prayer vigil, and thus we began losing the gains from our earlier victory.)

* * *

Now contrast the story above with the following (also true) story, from a spiritual warfare gathering in a southern city.

"Okay, everyone on your feet!" yelled the man on stage, with the gusto of a Marine drill sergeant. Approximately seven hundred people obediently jumped up.

"The Lord has given us the assignment tonight to pull down the spirit of pride from above our city! Can I hear an *Amen?*" The impassioned audience cried out in compliance.

"Everybody hold up your right hand!" Again, they followed the leader. (Haven't we all played that game?)

"Now I want you to grab that prince demon of pride by his slimy old tail. . . . Have you got it?"

The crowd, who until then had seemed like an intelligent-looking group, thundered back, *"Yes!"*

"On the count of three let's pull him down out of the heaven-lies . . . ready? One, two, three . . . PULL!"

They yanked with a shout of victory. The worship band caught up the theme. The entire place erupted in victorious celebration. *Celebration of what?* I wondered.

Across the aisle from me were three young children who had no idea what they were doing as they supposedly participated in "jerking down a demonic prince." Nearby was a frail-looking man who had a pack of cigarettes in his shirt pocket—he could barely catch his next breath for the next cheer. He didn't have victory over his habit, yet he was being told to assault territorial rulers? *Something's wrong with this picture.*

Why must the air war wait? As I've said, in this spiritual conflict the air war can't begin until the ground war is won. The ground war is the fight being waged in our own hearts and minds and in our relationships with others. Winning this war is neither fun nor exciting; we must win it in repentance, restitution, and reconciliation. We must never forget: The power that destroys satanic yokes is the Holy Spirit within us, not ourselves. As long as we demonstrate division, turfism, and self-centeredness, the Spirit will not empower us. Without the Spirit of God's anointing, we invite defeat. *It is our sin that provides strength for the satanic strongholds over our cities.*

The most pressing immediate need, for most of us, isn't to declare war on hell but to conquer our own sin. Until we repent of our pride, pursue personal integrity, and accept some accountability concerning spiritual battle, our impotent foolishness will do nothing to help the prayer movement and may eventually derail it.

We, the church, are the army of Jesus Christ, the Lord of Hosts and our Captain. But we're woefully out of shape. We lack effective commitment, organization, discipline, training, and endurance. Pastor: Protecting the sheep is a natural instinct for you. However, make sure you don't only see your people as sheep. You must also equip them to get off spiritual welfare and into spiritual warfare!

WARRING FOR TERRITORY

In chapters 5 and 6 we discussed the ground- and occult-level battlefields. This third battlefield, the territorial level, is in the heavenlies. Specifically, this is the strategic level, where Paul suggests we must stand against territorial prince demons (see Ephesians 6:12).

It takes two full days for Alice and me to teach on this subject. There's almost no way I can cover it in a shorter span. However, I almost feel I need to write two versions: one for the Western world and one for developing nations. We, in the West, have a pervasive and overriding anti-supernatural bias; most developing nations do not. For generations those believers wrestled with spirits, even long before many of them knew Christ.

I've heard George Otis Jr. refer to us as "people of the excluded middle." We accept the first heaven, which we can see; and the third heaven, where God dwells; but are reluctant to acknowledge the second heaven, where demonic rulers reside.

Satan's kingdom is real, and he's territorial. How do we know? For one thing, we have it in his own words: "I will be like the Most High" (Isaiah 14:14 KJV). He is trying to defeat and replace God, who Scripture teaches is *remarkably* territorial. It was God who laid the earth's foundations, marked off its dimensions, and laid its cornerstones; He fixed limits for the clouds and the seas; He set its doors and bars in place, and He said, *"This far you may come and no farther"* (Job 38:11; see also vv. 4–10; cf. Psalm 24:1–2; 74:17; 102:25).

Furthermore, unlike the omnipresent God, Satan isn't in all places at all times. To carry out his assignments and accomplish his plans, Satan *out of necessity* is territorial. He seeks to dominate world affairs, so he assigns his underlings to the kingdoms of the earth (see Matthew 4:8–9) and thereby exerts his strength. (*Note:* Satan rules men and nations as well as his demonic underlings with fear and intimidation.)

The devil's organization has proven to be highly effective. It was none other than Jesus who prophesied that the gates of hell would not be able to withstand the church. I've heard many different definitions of "the gates of hell." So I'll hazard a guess. We're told in the Old Testament that the elders, the judges, sat at the gates, and it was there that legal disputes were settled (e.g., see Proverbs 31:23). I believe "gates of hell" refers to "hell's elders," which would be Satan's territorial princes. After all, why would we focus on a lesser enemy?

Although the church has had two thousand years to dismantle and disarm the kingdom of darkness, it has spent too much time disputing lesser matters. Rather than challenge and wrestle against satanic leaders, we've wrestled one another.

The result is that *most of the men and women, boys and girls on this planet have yet to hear the name of Jesus spoken even once* (cf. 2 Corinthians 4:3–4).[2]

* * *

Satan's territorial victories involve nations, territories, and cities where he spiritually deafens and blinds groups of people lest they hear and respond to the gospel message (e.g., see Acts 16:16–26;

19:23–36; Ephesians 6:12). Satanic control of nations, just as with individuals, results from unrestrained sin. Herein the culture and/ or its leaders drift in darkness willingly until they—through whatever ways and means—establish contracts with darkness. At that point the devil puts territorial spirits in place, and God, who will not violate the will of men to have them serve Him, watches them yield their divinely given dominion to darkness.

> When the Lord has finished all his work against Mount Zion and Jerusalem, he will say, "I will punish the king of Assyria [typically referred to as Satan] for the willful pride of his heart and the haughty look in his eyes [the sin that caused Lucifer to fall].
> For he says: " 'By the strength of my hand I have done this, and by my wisdom, because I have understanding.
> I removed the boundaries of nations,
> I plundered their treasures;
> like a mighty one I subdued their kings.
> As one reaches into a nest, so my hand reached for the wealth of the nations;
> as men gather abandoned eggs,
> so I gathered all the countries;
> not one flapped a wing,
> or opened its mouth to chirp.' "
> (Isaiah 10:12–14)[3]

What can we learn from this passage? We learn that . . .

- Satan is a strong, prideful, arrogant being who has wisdom and understanding. Anyone who would rebel against Jehovah, face-to-face, in the glory of His fully manifested presence, is not to be taken lightly.
- Satan successfully removes the spiritual and physical

boundaries of the nations and plunders their treasures (the souls of men and women, boys and girls). He does this by provoking one nation to defeat another, then takes their wealth and their territory.

• Satan subdues "kings" (or leaders) by deceiving religious, political, and social leaders; as he steals their resources, no one sufficiently opposes him. (The greatest wealth of a nation is its next generation. "Gathering eggs" in America's case might well be our acceptance of abortion, the epidemic of fatherless children, and the prevalence of youthful addictions.)

• While Satan has done this, we (God's church) have not "flapped a wing, or opened our mouths to chirp." *We have not contended with the powers of darkness!*

THE SOLUTION

We have noted that Paul, in Ephesians 6, says that we are to put on God's armor so we can stand against the devil's schemes. In verse 12, we encounter a word that the *King James Version* renders as *wrestle;* in the *New International Version,* it's translated *struggle.*

> Our struggle is not against flesh and blood, but against the rulers, against the authorities, against the powers of this dark world and against the spiritual forces of evil in the heavenly realms.

Don't envision Greco-Roman wrestlers; instead, think of this in American football terms. Imagine a running back, ball cradled in his arms, charging toward the goal line. There are only seconds left; he must reach the end zone before the time expires for his team to win the game. In this illustration, the ball carrier represents us.

The opposing team represents the satanic structures, strategies, and beings amassed against us.

Yes, we must wrestle and struggle. But do not think for a second that wrestling or struggling is the point. The point is the play the quarterback has called, and the touchdown that will add six points to the scoreboard when the goal line is breached!

Occasionally I meet people who focus primarily on the enemy. Using my analogy, they only play *defense*, never taking their eyes, minds, and hearts off their opponent. We can't prevail against the devil if we're always on the defensive. In Matthew 16:18, foretelling the church's attack on the devil's kingdom, Jesus gives an *offensive* metaphor, exhorting us onward to *pro-action*. The gates of hell are statically struggling to withstand our concerted assault.

Jesus Christ, our quarterback, has called the play. It's called "The Great Commission" (see Matthew 28:19–20). The goal line to be crossed is a world to win. The score increases with each new believer who steps out of darkness and into the light. You cannot both please the Father and refuse to share Christ with others. There are no "silent witnesses"! You're not to be a spectator in this fight; you are called to be a combatant.

* * *

Jesus foretold that the church would do the works that He did (see John 14:12). And through the years since His ascension, every generation has. He also said the church would do "*greater* works," works the Father has reserved for her. This refers not to *quantity* of works but to *quality*, which implies "similar yet greater." I believe these works have to do with territorial spirits, those demonic elders that sit at hell's gates. Jesus said they would not be able to stand against us. But successfully assaulting those gates—and the rulers seated there—is no assignment for a divided, what's-in-it-for-me church.

The time has come for Christ's mature bride, arrayed in purity, standing in unity, to declare authoritatively to those long-entrenched princes of evil, *"No more! Enough is enough!"* We are seeing this happen in nation after nation around the world. Amazingly, the number of evangelical believers is growing at a rate three and a half times that of the world population![4]

A *massive* spiritual harvest is being reaped, nowhere more amazingly than in China.

Also, a few years ago I was blessed to be in São Paulo, Brazil, on the day of the International March for Jesus. The city had two and a half million people march for Jesus that day. It took five hundred U.S. cities to reach a total of two and a half million marchers!

Perhaps no one has invested as much time documenting this phenomenon than noted researcher George Otis Jr. of the Sentinel Group. Otis has spent years circling the globe with his video team, documenting the transformation of cities, territories, and nations. More than fifty million people, in more than one hundred fifty nations, on six continents, have viewed his *Transformations* videos in twenty-five languages.[5] Heaven celebrates!

SPIRITUAL MAPPING

During Operation Desert Storm, when the United States was trying to prevent Saddam Hussein from overtaking Kuwait (Iraq's tiny neighbor to the south) night after night we watched infrared-recorded video footage of military exercises carried out under cover of darkness. It was remarkable to see a missile leave a jet and find its way to a GPS-identified target—not just the building in which the enemy was hiding, but the very window that had been satellite-selected!

Similarly, God has given the church two powerful and precise tools to equip her for carrying out what may be the last great assault on the kingdom of darkness.

The first is the *prophetic ability* to hear God's voice. Through prophetic gifts and prophetic intercession, God is revealing realities previously unknown to us, directing our prayer assaults.

* * *

Alice was leading a prayer journey to Latvia shortly after the fall of the Soviet Union. Months before the team was formed and trained, before they determined their assignment, and before they flew to Latvia, she had a dream. In the dream God vividly showed her and her entire team standing at what she later would learn was a very historic place. Then God pointed out significant landmarks where prayer assignments eventually would be given.

Understand, six months before a team was formed, she had seen them. She wrote down what God showed her, and many months later we were standing at the very spot she had seen in her dream. I suggested that she put us in the order we were in when she saw us in the dream. And remarkably, when she began sharing with our guide the landmarks revealed in her dream, we learned they were exactly as she'd seen them. That is an example of prophetically hearing God's voice when receiving divine direction.

Over a period of several years, God revealed a warfare assignment to Alice that related to Israel. Interestingly, after she'd been journaling all God was showing her, one day her mother called and asked if she'd accompany her to Israel. Alice knew this was the assigned time to carry out her prayer mission.

Then Eraina Lothringer, one of our longtime intercessors, had a vision of Jerusalem. Eraina had never been to Israel, but she wrote specific—street by street, block by block—instructions for Alice to use after arriving. To Alice's surprise, an Israeli cab driver was able to use Eraina's instructions to arrive at a specific point God had revealed to her. Prophetic revelation, hearing God's voice, is a powerful tool for territorial prayer assignments. God speaks in many ways, including dreams, visions, Scripture, words of wisdom (unique applications of knowledge), and words of knowledge (knowledge beyond the natural; see 1 Corinthians 12:8).

* * *

The second powerful and precise tool is *spiritual mapping,* which involves researching, diagnosing, and responding to the spiritual dynamics in a given city, territory, or nation. The combination of what we call objective information (facts we obtain, for instance, through interviews and studies) and subjective impressions (e.g., revelation, words of knowledge, dreams, and visions) provides a compass with which we can discern the moral gateways between the spirit world and the material world. God reveals the nature, and at times even the names, of territorial spirits that govern regions so we can overturn their disorder and establish God's kingdom order.

The term *spiritual mapping* was coined by George Otis Jr., who has said there are *tools of the ages* and *tools of the age.* Tools of the *ages* are appropriate for every generation, including such things as prayer, fasting, faith, and love.

Tools of the *age* are implements God gives to a new generation to complete the task at hand. Spiritual mapping is an example of a tool revealed to our generation. Harold Caballeros, a Guatemalan pastor, says, "Spiritual mapping is to intercessors what X-rays are to doctors."[6]

* * *

Suppose I took a detailed map of my city to a library in order to research its criminal history. Let's say my city was founded in 1826. For starters, I could investigate Native American history for crimes or traumas that occurred prior to 1826.

Imagine I then discovered that a heathen temple once stood in what's now the city's northeast corner. I mark my map with a red X on that spot.

Suppose I learn next that, in 1897, a black man was lynched at a certain place. Another red X.

Perhaps in 1929, a serial rapist ravaged a specific neighborhood. I put Xs where the assaults occurred.

I would be doing this because every time a series of wrongs is committed, demonic (lower level) and territorial (higher level) spirits are attracted to its locales like bugs to a light. Remember: The continual sins of men and women are like signatures on a contract that finally assigns "the deed" over to satanic forces. After an area has been given to him, the enemy stakes his claim and begins operation. Can you see how spiritual mapping over a period of almost two hundred years might reveal sections of your city where Satan has had his greatest successes in defiling the land (e.g., see Leviticus 18:24–25, 27; Deuteronomy 21:22-23; 2 Kings 23:8; Isaiah 24:5; Jeremiah 2:7)?

(We could do the same with godly successes, marking where revivals and awakenings have occurred, where strong churches once stood, or still stand, and so forth. I've seen this done where a clear plastic sheet was used to represent each year that passed. Over a period of time, as the Xs begin to pile up, it becomes clear where the city's spiritually blessed parts are located.)

* * *

Going a step further, you'll likely find the areas that have suffered the most trauma to be the city's epicenter of poverty, crime, and corruption today. You'll probably discover that although many churches have been planted in that part (or those parts) of town, most haven't taken root.

Why? Because the land is defiled. Territorial spirits have claimed it and have been strengthened to do so by the sins people have committed there. The land needs to be cleansed before someone attempts to plant another church there. Yes, in terms of ownership, the earth is the Lord's (e.g., see Exodus 3:5; Psalm 24:1), but it becomes defiled by the sin of humankind.

Cleansing the land is to repent of the sins that have defiled it; Nehemiah provides an example. When he found Jerusalem in ruins, he repented of his sins, for the sins of his people, and even for his ancestor's sins. Nehemiah bore no guilt for the wrongs of others; conversely, he was identifying with them and apologizing to God for the damage they had wrought. This is "identificational repentance," through which someone "stands in the gap" through intercession (see Nehemiah 1:4–6).

Standing in the gap is to stand in prayer and pronounce, "Thy kingdom come, Thy will be done on earth as it is in heaven." Vital, effective prayer stands between heaven and earth—between what God wants to do here and what is being done here. As prayer warriors, we hear our instructions from heaven; then we pray, and we declare them on earth.

When I teach, I often ask the question, "Can you finish this

Scripture verse? 'I looked for a man...who would...stand before me in the gap . . . '" There are lots of guesses, and the most common is "but I found none." That is indeed part of the verse, but apparently many of us have missed the phrase in between: *"on behalf of the land"* (see Ezekiel 22:30). God was searching for someone to stand in the gap on behalf of the land. Just as Nehemiah rebuilt Jerusalem's walls physically, so our cities must be rebuilt spiritually. Colossians 1:20 teaches us that Jesus died to "reconcile all things unto himself" (KJV). Any place on earth can be defiled by sin, and it can be reconciled to God through the blood of Christ.

THE ADVANCING KINGDOM

I will give you the treasures of darkness,
riches stored in secret places,
so that you may know that I am the LORD,
the God of Israel. (Isaiah 45:3)

In Isaiah's day, Old Testament armies battled physical foes. New Testament armies (the purified, unified church) are to battle in the heavenlies under the command of Jesus Christ, the Lord of Hosts. This last battle will be directed against Satan's headquarters in the second heaven, the gates of which, Jesus prophesied, shall not prevail against us (see Matthew 16:18).

Christ's bride, the church, fighting from her knees all around the world, is already ushering in the kingdom of God and displacing the kingdom of darkness. She's pushing back forces of evil for periods of time, allowing millions the opportunity to hear and respond to the gospel for the first time. We're seeing the fulfillment of Psalm 2:8 as we ask our Father for the nations. And peoples of the nations are coming to Him!

Some say, "Psalm 2:8 is a prophetic verse about the Son of God. It says *He'll* one day ask the Father for the nations as *His* inheritance." True. But have you considered that there's more? Something the prophetic psalmist couldn't possibly have understood when he was writing?

We also are sons of God, and joint-heirs with Jesus. His inheritance belongs to each of us (individually) just as it belongs to Him.

Beyond that, we are Christ's body. In the past two decades believers worldwide have focused their praying, crying out to the Father for the nations. It stands to reason that the Son's body on earth will do what the Son likewise is doing as He's seated at the Father's right hand.

God *is* giving us the nations. More people have been born again in Iran during the past twenty years than in the past two thousand years combined! The greatest-ever harvest of souls is happening today in China, where for thousands of years the dragon (biblically symbolic of Satan) has been worshiped. The gates of hell are *not* prevailing against the church.

* * *

Once more, this war for souls is being waged simultaneously on two fronts: There is the air war, and there is the ground war. Spiritual warriors in developing nations are typically first-generation Christians. Many are the first in their families to accept Christ. The majority of their warfare prayer is focused on the air conflict—where the prince and power of the air (Satan—see Ephesians 2) and his minions (territorial principalities) are headquartered. Strategic warriors are identifying and demolishing strongholds with outstanding results: Tens of thousands are being born again every day.

To conquer Satan's army, we must *become* the army of God. To defeat satanic forces, we must *become* a force—a force for God's kingdom. In too many cases we have elevated spiritual gifts above spiritual fruit. Some like to measure themselves and others by whether or not they share the same spiritual gift rather than by whether or not they're bearing the fruit of the Spirit and living Christlike lives.

It's time we forsake spiritual pride and acknowledge how little real evidence there is of God's Spirit at work in our hearts, our families, and our cities.

Many of us have determined that the measure of our spiritual depth is seen in our lives—in ourselves. In actuality, *the true measure of our spiritual depth is seen in our relationships with others.* Let's refocus on our relationships. We cannot show a lost world how to be reconciled to God unless and until we are reconciled to each other.

God will never find our offering acceptable until our relationships honor Him.

If you are offering your gift at the altar and there remember that your brother has something against you, leave your gift there in front of the altar. First go and be reconciled to your brother; then come and offer your gift. (Matthew 5:23–24)

Consider also your relationship to your city. Too many of us speak more about what we *don't like* about our cities than what we *do like.* Your city is your God-given assignment. Love your city. Speak blessings over your city. Never curse the land God has given you.

INSIGHTS TO REMEMBER

- Warfare music, though appropriate at the right time, should never be used to replace praise and worship.

- When we hit the target in spiritual warfare, we can expect God to provide confirmation, and some measure of victory.

- It is our sin that provides strength for the satanic strongholds over our cities.

- Satan is territorial because (a) God is and (b) unlike God, he isn't omnipresent and is relegated to one place at a time.

- Satan is attempting to remove the boundaries of nations and plunder their treasures.

- We wrestle with darkness to complete the Great Commission.

- The number of evangelical Christians is growing at the rate of three and a half times that of the world's population!

- *Spiritual mapping* is the process of researching, diagnosing, and responding to the spiritual dynamics in a given city, territory, or nation.

- *Cleansing the land* is a process of repenting for the sins that have defiled it.

- This last battle will be directed against Satan's headquarters in the second heaven, the gates of which, Jesus promised, will be unable to withstand the church's assault.

- To conquer Satan's army, we must *become* the army of God.

THE WARRIOR'S HEART

It's been well over half a century since America was totally immersed in war. Neither Korea nor Vietnam brought the U.S. into unilateral engagement as did World Wars I and II. We mentioned that Desert Storm, primarily an air war, almost seemed over before it began. The nation appeared unified when the current fight against Islamic terrorism began, but as time has passed, an increasing thirst for power and control has threatened to divide our people and weaken our resolve.

Some Americans recognize the significance of the war against terrorism; others don't have a clue. Nonetheless, many do not recognize that *this war is an ideological war, a spiritual battle that can never be won with guns and missiles.* The same phenomenon is mirrored in the spiritual war against Satan and his hordes. Some Christians recognize the significance of the unseen warfare that rages around us, while others either don't get it or won't acknowledge it.

Americans know little about death and destruction compared to the rest of the world. We know relatively little about fighting and violence, and we generally practice "live and let live." As Christians, too, most of us were raised to practice love and kindness. Very few of us, at present, have the heart of a warrior.

THE ARMOR OF GOD

In Ephesians 6, we're told:

Put on the full armor of God, so that when the day of evil comes, you may be able to stand your ground, and after you have done everything, to stand. Stand firm then, with the *belt of truth* buckled around your waist, with the *breastplate of righteousness* in place, and with your *feet fitted with the readiness that comes from the gospel of peace*. In addition to all this, take up the *shield of faith,* with which you can extinguish all the flaming arrows of the evil one. Take the *helmet of salvation* and the *sword of the Spirit,* which is the word of God. And pray in the Spirit on all occasions with all kinds of prayers and requests. With this in mind, be alert and always keep on praying for all the saints. (vv. 13–18, emphasis mine)

The most common instruction I've heard regarding this passage is that we are to awaken every morning and "pray on" God's armor. I disagree. I believe the *armor* Paul refers to is descriptive of the *life we're living* and, thus increasingly, as time passes, the life we've lived—not a prayer we've prayed.

Notice, for example, that the book of Ephesians doesn't *begin* referring to warfare; it *ends* with warfare. The first five chapters deal with how we are to live.

When I was born again at age five and a half (the "halves" were important back then!), I put on the helmet *of* salvation. It was then that I trusted Christ as my personal Savior.

As I've read, memorized, meditated upon, and used the Word of God, I've put on the belt *of* truth and taken up the sword *of* the Spirit. The sword *of* the Spirit—the Word *of* God—is our only offensive weapon. If you've not taken it up, you are unarmed. There are no shortcuts. *You can't "pray it on."*

As I've received Christ's righteousness and allowed Him to live His life in and through me, I've clothed myself with the breastplate *of* righteousness. There is the righteousness *of* Christ that's imputed to me, and the righteousness that I must live out. Together they form my breastplate.

Since elementary school I've openly shared my faith in Jesus as a witness, a soul winner. In this way I've put on my "gospel shoes." That is, my feet are fitted with the preparation *of* the gospel *of* peace.

As I've been tested and tried, I've learned to trust *the Lord.* That's where I've received the shield *of* faith. Because I continue to live it out, my shield grows day by day.

I've noticed that many of us focus on the metaphor rather than the message. We see the belt, the breastplate, the shoes, the shield, the helmet, and the sword. We should be focusing on truth, righteousness, soul winning, faith, salvation, and the Word of God!

Anyone who denies the truth, lives unrighteously, shrinks from sharing the good news, is fearful and isolated, continually questions his salvation, and doesn't know God's Word isn't prepared to engage in spiritual warfare. Do you understand what I'm trying to say? God's armor goes onto us—and *we grow into it*—as we abide in Him and increase in faith.

Yes—absolutely, certainly, always *pray.* Just don't make the error of thinking that we become mature, seasoned veterans of faith either by merely asking for that to happen or by merely declaring that it is happening.

BECOMING A SPIRITUAL SOLDIER

In prayer one day the Lord asked me a puzzling question: "Eddie, do you hate Satan?" Go ahead, ask yourself the same: *Do* you hate him? We know we should—but do we? The condition of our world saddens us, and we're unsettled by the pain and misery that evil causes. But do we actually *hate* the prince of darkness?

I had never allowed myself to hate anyone or anything—except for Brussels sprouts (not little Belgian children—*the vegetable!*). After all, I'd believed that hatred is sinful. Jesus says to love our enemies and pray for those who persecute us (see Matthew 5:43–44). Paul reminds us to feed our enemies and give them something to drink (see Romans 12:20).

I remember the difficult question a young boy once asked me: "Pastor Eddie, God says we should love our enemies, right?"

"That's right," I assured him.

"Then does God love the devil?" he pressed. (That suddenly seemed to me like a perfect time for our Sunday school class to take a break!)

While hating evil and hating sin, we are still to love people— even sinners (see Romans 5:8). What about Satan? Satan is pure, unadulterated evil. He is unrepentant and unable to be regenerated; his eternal doom is already set. Conversely, the most evil person in this world *can* repent and be reborn.

* * *

Paul also wrote, "Hate what is evil" (Romans 12:9). Sure, I disliked the devil, but did I *hate* him? Paul continued: "Never be lacking in zeal, but keep your spiritual fervor, serving the Lord" (v. 11). Had I ever been enraged at Satan? Where was my fiery zeal? I realized I didn't have the heart of a warrior. At the same time, a warrior was exactly what God was calling me to become.

I remembered that after being sworn in to the U.S. Navy, I was sent to boot camp in San Diego. Upon arrival at the base, I was informed that over the next eleven weeks I'd be transformed into a warrior. Trust me—I was not a warrior; I was a college student. I was a green recruit with no idea what to expect.

They introduced me to a diminutive, wiry-looking sailor twice my age. He was a highly decorated war veteran, and he was to be my drill instructor. His job was to impart his battle experience and hard-won knowledge to me, and he took his job seriously! During those eleven weeks, he was a key part of adding layers of toughness to us.

One day during my quiet time, as I wrestled with thoughts concerning conflict between good and evil, God again revealed to me that I didn't have the heart of a spiritual warrior. He led me to the Psalms for some basic training. David, another highly decorated warrior, was to be my *spiritual* drill sergeant.

When you read about his life and read the psalms he wrote, you will notice how David grew into his warfare assignment. We will need to do the same. We must understand that our authority over evil relates to (1) who we are in Christ and (2) the maturity we develop through years of warfare and victory. We see a description of this development in Hebrews 5:12–14:

> Though by this time you ought to be teachers, you need some-
> one to teach you the elementary truths of God's word all over

again. You need milk, not solid food! Anyone who lives on milk, being still an infant, is not acquainted with the teaching about righteousness. But solid food is for the mature, who by constant use have trained themselves to distinguish good from evil.

Read also verse 14 from other translations:

[The mature are those] who by reason of use have their senses exercised to discern good and evil. (KJV)

[Mature is the person] who has developed by experience his power to discriminate between what is good and bad for him. (PHILLIPS)

[The mature] by reason of habit have their organs of perception well trained. (ROTHERHAM)

[The mature are] those who by constant practice have their spiritual faculties carefully trained. (WNT)

This pattern of distinguishing, confronting, and defeating evil builds our faith. It is faith—faith based on who Jesus is, and thus who we are—that strengthens our authority.

* * *

As a young shepherd boy, David had killed a lion and a bear with his bare hands to protect his father's sheep (1 Samuel 17:33–35). Later, without armor or intimidation, he killed Goliath with a single stone from his sling (vv. 48–49). Beginning as King Saul's armor-bearer (16:21; 18:2), he was promoted to captain over one thousand soldiers (18:5).

As inconceivable as it might seem, he purchased his wife Michal from her father, Saul, for the price of one hundred Philistine foreskins. Philistine foreskins weren't for sale at the local market, you understand. He didn't buy them on eBay. *He won them in battle.*

God honored David's warrior heart, and the young man rose to such prominence that his position was beneath only those of Abner, captain of the hosts, and of Jonathan, Saul's son. *David became a man of war and a man after God's own heart* (13:14). David's development of experience and faith came from one fight to the next.

God's kingdom represents a family. God is our Father, and Christ is our brother. But God's kingdom is also an army. Don't forget that we serve a God of war. And remember that Jesus Christ, Lord of Hosts, is Commander in Chief.

If you walk with God only as His child or as His bride, then you are missing a significant dimension of your relationship with Him. In addition, you're missing the military assignments He wants to give you. Someone's life, perhaps someone's family, or even someone's nation, may be hanging in the balance where your faithful obedience to the Lord's warfare assignment will be the determining force. Can you be counted on?

A NEW VOCABULARY

It wasn't long before I noticed the way David, my ancient drill instructor, prayed against his enemies. Through this, the Lord showed me I needed a new vocabulary.

That wasn't the first time God had done this. Several years earlier He'd sent me to the Psalms to learn how to praise Him. That's right. I searched the Psalms for phrases David used to celebrate God. You see, before that I'd never developed a praise vocabulary. Now I was to learn a warfare-prayer vocabulary.

This new "weapon" wasn't (and isn't) to be used against people. It's true that David prayed against people who were his foes; he prayed what we call "imprecatory prayers," which means, literally, that he prayed curses. In the Old Testament, sinners were often put to death. However, in the New Testament, Jesus died for them—for us . . . for all of us. And He made clear to us that our highest calling is to love God and love others, granting grace and forgiveness just as He has showered grace and forgiveness upon us. (See Matthew 22:37–39; John 13:34–35; cf. Leviticus 20:10 and John 8:1–11.)

Now, because of Christ's sacrifice of atonement, we are to bless others and pray *for* their salvation, even wicked people (see Matthew 5:43–44). We are to pray that mercy will triumph over judgment (see James 2:13). Our warfare vocabulary is to equip us for battle against Satan and his minions, spiritual beings for whom there is no redemption.

* * *

Stop for a moment and ask yourself this question: "What is my most pressing prayer concern?" When you have it, look back at the prayers you've been praying about this problem. Have you been praying against people, or against the kingdom of darkness? I've been in meetings where I've heard people praying for God to do bad things to "problem people." *Problem people are not our enemies!*

Returning to David and the Psalms, I wrote out many warfare-related phrases and referred to my list at times when I prayed. This helped me express my heart as I rose up in warfare prayer against the kingdom of darkness, fighting for revival, pushing for spiritual awakening, defending the helpless, and so forth.

As an example, here are a few phrases (mostly paraphrased)

from just a few psalms. As you read through them, evaluate your own capacity for warfare.

> Confuse the counsel of the enemy
> May their trees yield no fruit
> May their leaves wither and die
> May they, like chaff, be blown away by the wind
> May their way perish before them. (Psalm 1)

Before we go any further, let's take phrases from this psalm and consider how you could utilize them in warfare prayer. It might sound something like this:

Father God, I come to you on behalf of the young people in our city. This rash of suicides among high school students is breaking my heart. I pray that you will confuse the counsel of the devil. Please cause all of the efforts of the demons who are deceiving these young people to cease bearing fruit, to wither, and to die. Lord, let these spirits of suicidal death be like chaff, blown away by the wind. Cause their plans to come to naught. Deliver these children from their evil influence.

> Break the enemies' chains on us and throw off their fetters
> Laugh and scoff at them, O Lord
> Rebuke them in your anger and terrify them in your wrath
> Proclaim to the enemy the truth concerning your Son
> Give the nations to Jesus as His inheritance
> Give the peoples to Jesus as His purchased possession
> Rule over the enemy with an iron scepter
> Dash them to pieces like pottery
> Strike them with fear and trembling
> Destroy them in their way. (Psalm 2)

You are a shield around me
I will not fear the tens of thousands drawn up against me
Strike the enemy on the jaw and shatter his teeth
Arise, O Lord! (Psalm 3)

Destroy the enemies' lies and deceit
May we not trust a word from their mouths
Protect us from the destruction that is in their hearts
Declare them guilty, O Lord
Banish them for their many sins; they have rebelled against you
Let their intrigues be their downfall. (Psalm 5)

Rebuke the enemy in your anger
and discipline them in your wrath
May they be worn out because of their groaning
May their eyes grow weak with sorrow
May they fail
May the enemy be ashamed and dismayed
May they be turned back in sudden disgrace. (Psalm 6)

Pursue and overtake them, O Lord
Tear them like a lion and rip them to pieces
Trample their life to the ground like dust
Rise up in rage against the enemy
Arise, O Lord, and decree justice
Bring to an end their violence
Do not relent, O Lord
Sharpen your sword
Bend and string your bow
Prepare your deadly weapons
Make ready your flaming arrows
Cause them to fall into the pits they have dug
Cause their trouble to recoil on themselves
Cause their violence to come down on their own heads. (Psalm 7)

Silence the foe and the avenger
Rebuke the enemy
Destroy the wicked
Cause endless ruin to overtake them
Uproot their cities
Cause even the memory of them to perish
Avenge the blood of the innocent
Cause the enemy to become ensnared
by the work of their own hands
Let not the enemy prevail
Strike them in terror. (Psalm 8)

Lift up your hand, O God
Do not forget the helpless
Break their arms, O God
Cause them to perish from the land
Call them to account for their wickedness. (Psalm 10)

Rain fiery coals and burning sulfur upon them
Cause a scorching wind to come upon them. (Psalm 11)

Lord, cut off their flattering lips and boastful tongues. (Psalm 12)

Cause their sorrow to increase. (Psalm 16)

Rise up, O Lord, confront them and bring them down
Rescue us from the wicked by your sword. (Psalm 17)

Hear my voice, O Lord
Be angry with my enemy
Let smoke rise from your nostrils
Let a consuming fire and burning coals come from your mouth

Part the heavens and come down
Let your voice thunder from heaven, O Most High
Shoot your arrows and scatter your enemies
Rout them with great bolts of lightning
Rebuke them, O Lord
Blast them with the breath of your nostrils
Pursue the enemy and overtake them
Crush them so that they cannot rise
Cause our adversaries to bow at our feet
Cause them to turn their backs in flight
Beat them as fine as dust borne on the wind
May they lose heart and cringe before you, O Lord
May they come trembling from their strongholds. (Psalm 18)

Seize the enemy with your strong right hand
Swallow them in your wrath and consume them with your fire
Destroy them utterly from the earth
Make them turn their backs
as you take aim at them with your bow. (Psalm 21)

Cause them to be poured out like water
Cause their bones to be out of joint
Melt their hearts like wax within them
Cause their strength to dry up like a potsherd. (Psalm 22)

Notice words like *crush, scorch, rage, blast, seize.* Do these seem too violent, too unkind . . . just too much? Remember, it was Jesus who said, "From the days of John the Baptist until now, the kingdom of heaven has been forcefully advancing, and forceful men lay hold of it" (Matthew 11:12).

FROM CIVILIANS TO SERGEANTS

When it comes to spiritual warfare today, there are many civilians in the church. These folks attend the services but have yet to be born again. Of that group, some know they are lost and are trying to find solutions for their condition. Others don't know they are lost and have never really received revelation unto salvation.

Either way, they aren't wearing the uniform—salvation, the robe of righteousness—Christ's righteousness. They are still clothed in their own righteousness, which is no better than "filthy rags" to God (see Isaiah 64:6). No wonder they're easy prey for the enemy.

Many in the church *have* been born again and are saved from eternity in hell apart from God, but they nonetheless are oblivious to the war that rages around them. They remind me of myself the day I stepped off the bus in San Diego—a *raw recruit*. In some cases these raw recruits, not yet trained, are watching helplessly as their worlds are caving in around them, and they have no idea what they should do about it.

Others, like spiritual draft dodgers, recognize there's a spiritual war and know that God has called them yet they refuse to accept their responsibility in His army. Laziness, pride, fear, or perhaps worry for what others will think of them prevents many from engaging the enemy on behalf of themselves and others.

Some are AWOL (Absent Without Leave); they have received some warfare training and had a few battlefield experiences, but for one reason or another, perhaps the resulting backlash, they've given up the fight.

Perhaps the POWs (Prisoners of War) are saddest of all. They're born again, but the enemy still holds them captive. Addicted to alcohol, nicotine, sex, drugs (legal/illegal), or other harmful things, they're stuck in bondage and offer little testimony for Jesus. Having been set free by His sacrifice, when they should be soaring in the heavenlies, they have remained earthbound in spiritual chains. When they could and should be experiencing abundant life, they languish instead, shackled in the devil's dungeon.

And among those who really are warriors, some are wounded and in need of healing, and some are exhausted and battle-weary. They need what the military calls R&R—rest and relaxation.

*　*　*

One of the reasons I'm writing to you today is to help you identify who you are, where you are in the kingdom, and where the Lord wants you to be. You see, the day I graduated from boot camp I was given my orders; this was my first military assignment. At that moment I knew who I was—a sailor in the United States Navy. And I knew where I was going—aboard the USS *Lynde McCormick* (DDG-8), a guided missile destroyer in the Pacific. Seek to learn both your identity and your assignment!

May the heavenly Father make us wise, forceful men and women who will despise Satan and his minions, the enemies here only to rob and to murder and to wreck.

May He give us warriors' hearts so that we, with Jesus, can effectively destroy the works of the devil (see 1 John 3:8).

May He reveal to us *who we truly are* in Christ.

May He make our assignments clear and find us willing to accept them.

Jesus said, "I tell you the truth, anyone who has faith in me will do what I have been doing. He will do even greater things than these, because I am going to the Father" (John 14:12).

Let it be.

INSIGHTS TO REMEMBER

- Some Christians recognize the significance of the unseen war that rages around us, while others don't get it or won't acknowledge it.

- God's armor is descriptive of the life we're living and, increasingly, the life we've lived.

- God's armor goes onto us—and we *grow into it*—as we abide in Him and increase in faith.

- God tells us that we are to hate what is evil.

- Like King David, we too must grow into our warfare assignments.

- Distinguishing, confronting, and defeating evil builds our faith.

- God's kingdom represents a family. But God's kingdom is also an army.

- In the Old Testament, God routinely killed sinners. In the New Testament, He died for them!

CHAPTER 9

THE REAL POWER

It was early morning, and the fog was still hanging mysteriously near the forest floor surrounding our northwest Houston home. Slowly I began driving to the church where I was to address a large group of women on the subject of spiritual warfare.

As I rolled up to a stop sign, something caught my eye. High above the pavement, precariously balanced on an electrical wire, was a squirrel. Tilting forward and backward, swaying first to the left, then to the right, it carefully inched its way across the street, using its furry tail as a tightrope walker might use a parasol.

The amazing squirrel was midway across when out of the fog came a crazed mockingbird. The Texas state bird, only about ten inches in length, is known to be fierce and combative in any threatening situation. It will go after offenders both small and large.

Like a fighter plane, the mockingbird strafed the startled

squirrel, pecking it on the head. A bit dazed, the assaulted rodent gathered its composure, turned cautiously, and aimed for the other side of the street.

As you can see, it doesn't take much to entertain me. Early for my meeting, I turned off the engine, climbed out of my car, and sat on the hood to watch this breathtaking aerial act. It was better than the circus!

Again and again, the mockingbird would circle, then dive out of the fog and strike the confused squirrel on the head with its sharp beak. After each attack the squirrel would reel, find its balance, and desperately try to reach the opposite side.

Finally, in what seemed to me a risky maneuver, the squirrel lunged for the closest electrical pole. Then it raced down, headfirst, and shot into a bush. All the while, the mockingbird continued its relentless attack.

The last thing I saw in my rearview mirror as I drove away was that bird diving into the bush for one more strike against the squirrel.

YOU ARE DANGEROUS!

At the conference, I relayed the story of the mockingbird and the squirrel. Then I asked the audience, "When it comes to spiritual warfare, how many of you can relate to that squirrel?" Perhaps recalling the spiritual migraines they had received from the enemy, almost without exception they nodded and raised their hands.

Leaning across the lectern, I said, "Not me. I relate to the mockingbird. God didn't put me here to get headaches from Satan; He put me here to *give* Satan headaches! *I am dangerous; and so are you!*"

It's true. Where Satan is concerned, if you're in Christ and Christ is in you, you are dangerous! Too many believers today have more faith in Satan's ability to steal, kill, and destroy than they have faith in Christ's ability to destroy the works of the devil. As the Father sent Christ, even so Christ sends us into this world to pull down satanic strongholds, to wreak havoc on evil, and to see the kingdom of God displace the kingdom of darkness (see Luke 10:19).

But we do this only as directed. Remember, we're not generals (decision-makers). We are ambassadors. We are to say and to do what Christ is saying and doing. In that context, what we say and do carries Christ's authority. It's as if *He said it!*

This is based on the "power of attorney" Jesus has given to us (see John 14:13–14). It's not a carte-blanche authority; we are not to use the name of Jesus as if it were a magic wand. We are to use His name when we are saying what He wants said and doing what He wants done. After all, we are saying and/or doing it on His behalf.

How do we know whether or not He approves? That, friend, is one of the most difficult aspects of ministry. The quick and easy answer is we know it's to be said or done when we are anointed to say or do it. The anointing of God comes on us and empowers us. Without it, we're simply shadow boxing.

John says it all in 1 John 4:17: "In this world we are like him." After all, we are Christ's body. He *lives* in His body!

As I mentioned in chapter 2, Satan fell as a result of the rebellion he led against God in heaven. As his punishment, God deported him to earth. You see, for anyone who has known the glories of heaven, anything less than heaven is severe punishment (see Mark 1:23–26).

In Jesus' encounter with Gadera's demons in Matthew 8:28–34, they asked if He had come to torment them before their time.

His answer was most assuredly yes (see 1 John 3:8). It's true; there will come a time of perfected punishment for them (Revelation 20:10). However, their punishment has already begun, and we have the privilege of assisting in carrying out the sentence against these wicked workers of iniquity.

God didn't leave us here to survive as "spiritual squirrels," sitting passively or, worse yet, balancing precariously on the tightrope of life, praying for protection. No! We're not mere survivors. God says we're even more than conquerors; we're *overcomers* (see Romans 8:37; 1 John 4:4). Someone who's more than a conqueror is a super-conqueror. So we've been made overcoming super-conquerors through Christ!

It's not our job to hold on with hope. We're here to fight on with faith. God put us here to be His mockingbirds. Through our faithful obedience to Jesus Christ, we can give Satan holy headaches. We're to be his worst nightmare, and the gates of hell *shall not* prevail.[1]

* * *

A woman once told me that she had rigged up her home with multiple cassette players. "Why?" I asked.

"To keep the enemy away," she explained.

To keep the enemy away? I thought. *Why would that keep the enemy away?*

Perhaps she was reminded of David's harp-playing that made King Saul's demon flee. I suspect, however, that it wasn't beautiful music from David's harp that drove the evil spirit from Saul. Although no one knows exactly what David's harp looked like, archeological drawings from coins and cave walls depict a crude instrument shaped like the letter *H*, with a solid bottom and from three to ten strings. Biblical archeologists have traced that yoke-shaped harp back about four thousand years.

My college major was music composition and arranging. Believe me: You'd not find the sounds of a Davidic harp entreating. More likely you'd find it a bit irritating. After all, remember: Satan is described as once having been heaven's worship leader. Music would be no problem.

No. When David played the harp it was more than music—he engaged in wholehearted worship. When he drew near to God, God drew near to him. When he played, God showed up. It's *God's presence* that evil spirits can't stand!

There's certainly nothing wrong with filling your home, your car, or your office with good music. It honors the Lord and warms the heart. But if you do it superstitiously, you may as well forget it.

Besides, I'm not looking for a demon-free zone in which to live. Christ certainly had none—He seemed to run into demons at every turn. After all, *God prepares my table in the presence of my enemies* (see Psalm 23). I'm to be so secure in Christ, so certain of my position in Him, so convinced of who He is to me and who I am to Him, that I will fearlessly eat in full view of the devil and his demons and not be intimidated.

* * *

Our youngest son, Bryan, has always been quite sensitive spiritually. He was about fifteen when one morning he emerged from his room and said, "Dad, a strange thing happened to me last night. I was almost asleep when I rolled over and saw that my entire ceiling was covered with demonic beings. They were snarling, sneering, and smiling at me."

"What did you do?" I asked.

"Like you and Mom have taught me, I asked the heavenly Father to make them go away."

"And what did God say?"

"He said no."

"'No'? Did you ask Him why?"

"Yes sir. God said, 'Bryan, I want you to let them watch you sleep.'"

"So what did you do?" I asked.

"Dad, I rolled over and fell asleep."

(Can you imagine the disappointment and defeat of a band of demons who've been sent to harass a young prophet of God when, after seeing their most intimidating snarls, he falls asleep on them?)

I said, "Bryan, go get your Bible and turn to Psalm 3." He did. "Now, read it to me."

> "God! Look! Enemies past counting!
>   Enemies sprouting like mushrooms,
>   Mobs of them all around me, roaring their mockery:
>   'Hah! No help for him from God!'
>
> "But you, GOD, shield me on all sides;
>   You ground my feet, you lift my head high;
>   With all my might I shout up to God,
>   His answers thunder from the holy mountain.
>
> "I stretch myself out. I sleep.
>   Then I'm up again—rested, tall and steady,
>   Fearless before the enemy mobs
>   Coming at me from all sides.

"Up, GOD! My God, help me!
   Slap their faces,
   First this cheek, then the other,
   Your fist hard in their teeth!

"Real help comes from GOD.
   Your blessing clothes your people!" (THE MESSAGE)

"Bryan," I said, "God allowed you to experience Psalm 3 last night."

* * *

Oh, I know. Some would say, "You shouldn't allow your experiences to determine your theology." But as a friend of mine would say, "Why? So a lack of experience can determine it instead?" The apostle Peter's noonday rooftop vision of a sheet containing unclean animals radically changed his theology (see Acts 10:9–23). Until that moment he'd wrongly concluded that only Jews could be born again. Thank God that Peter had been wrong. And thank God that he allowed his experience to contribute to his beliefs: "God does not show favoritism but accepts men from every nation who fear him and do what is right" (vv. 34-35).

There certainly is value in purifying your home or workplace. Alice and I wrote two books in which we address the need to go through our possessions routinely and rid ourselves of things that are contrary to God's nature.[2] The point of doing this, though, isn't based on a motivation of fear. It's about cleansing our homes to make them comfortable dwellings for the Holy Spirit.

Any home where Christ is honored will have an occasional demonic *visitation*. What you don't want is for it to become a demonic *habitation*.

BINDING AND LOOSING

One night in a Texas bar, I was witnessing with Jim, a full-time crusade evangelist, when suddenly a huge trucker took offense at Jim's soul-winning style. He jumped to his feet, grabbed Jim by the collar, and growled, "If you mention Jesus one more time I'm gonna—"

Having bowed his neck and jutted his jaw, Jim interrupted and said firmly, "I bind you in the name of Jesus!"

At that point I intervened. "Brother Jim, if it's a demon that's provoking this man, you might be in luck. But if it's his flesh . . . he's gonna kill you!"

* * *

The right person at the right time—that is, in God's timing—can bind a demon. But we do not have the authority to bind other people. To engage in effective spiritual warfare, we must know the applications and limitations of binding and loosing.

Suppose you're driving carelessly; the sound of a siren and the sight of spinning colored lights alert you to the fact that you've exceeded the speed limit. The first thing you do is pull over to the side of the road.

Now suppose that the uniformed officer who steps from the squad car and makes his way to your driver's-side window stands less than five feet tall and, wringing wet, couldn't weigh more than 120 pounds. What do you do?

You do exactly what he tells you to do. Not because you fear him; you could overpower him, physically. It's because, with his uniform and badge, you recognize his authority, which is backed up by the power of the government agency that authorizes him.

Some have mistakenly seen binding and loosing as simply a matter of power. Know this: You will never have the *power* to bind and loose unless and until you have the *authority* to do so. If you have the authority, the kingdom of darkness will know it.

* * *

The building was filled with excited Christians from five or six local churches. They had named this event "Bringing Balance to Spiritual Warfare." The worship band was amazing, though at one point the praise was so loud it could have peeled the paint off the walls!

The host pastor introduced me with "a Pentecostal flair." I trotted up the steps of the stage, dropped my Bible on the pulpit, and yelled, *"HOW MANY OF YOU HAVE THE POWER TO BIND SATAN TONIGHT, IN THE NAME OF JESUS?"*

It seemed the entire place jumped to its feet; people were throwing both hands in the air, and many were dancing in place as they cheered and screamed, "I can! I can!" The guitar did a riff, the drums did a roll, and the sax played a run. It was holy bedlam for a moment or so.

"Please be seated," I urged them quietly. Eventually they settled down.

Then I leaned across the pulpit and calmly asked, "Would one of you please do that? Would one of you please bind the devil right now and put an end to child abuse, abortion, murder, war, sickness, disease, and crime? Anyone? I know all of you *can* do it. Now I'm asking you *to* do it."

I waited. No one moved an inch. Hardly anyone breathed.

I continued, "If you can bind Satan, but *won't* do it, then you become his accomplice. Will someone *please* bind him?"

After an uncomfortable few seconds I said, "We have a slogan in Texas for folks like you. We'd say, 'It's time you either put up or . . . '" And of course they all finished the sentence for me.

All of our bravado is useless unless it's backed up with a basis in fact. And the fact is you and I cannot bind the devil unless God instructs, equips, and anoints us to do so. We see this actually happen in Revelation 20.

> I saw an Angel descending out of Heaven. He carried the key to the Abyss and a chain—a huge chain. He grabbed the Dragon, that old Snake—the very Devil, Satan himself!—chained him up for a thousand years, dumped him into the Abyss, slammed it shut and sealed it tight. No more trouble out of him, deceiving the nations—until the thousand years are up. After that he has to be let loose briefly. (vv. 1–3 THE MESSAGE)

ON EARTH AS IN HEAVEN

Peter Wagner points out that God is synchronizing earth with heaven. We're all familiar with the phrase from the model prayer Jesus taught His disciples: "Thy kingdom come, thy will be done on earth as it is in heaven." In this one sentence we learn an important key. Our assignment as heaven's ambassadors is about seeing the earth transformed as the kingdom of God *displaces* the kingdom of darkness. As Christ showed, one way this transaction occurs is through prayer. We are to ask God, perhaps daily, that His kingdom displace Satan's rule on the earth.

Another way this synchronization occurs is through what spiritual warriors refer to as "binding and loosing." Wagner writes:

Our *New King James* translation [of Matthew 18:18], "Whatever you bind on earth will be bound in heaven," fails to convey an extremely significant nuance of the original Greek. The more literal translation would be: "Whatever you bind on earth *will have been bound* in heaven and whatever you loose *will have been* loosed in heaven." This means that an essential synchronization exists between the activities on earth and activities in heaven. And it establishes the crucial sequence of: heaven *first*, then earth.[3]

In my travels across America and around the world, I spend a great deal of time with God's praying people. Many intercessors feel that spiritual warfare prayer is their primary calling. However, while they understand the necessity and the practice of binding and loosing, some haven't known about this process of synchronization. Although the intercessors' intentions have been good, their results often have been less than satisfactory. Unfortunately, they've assumed that if they bind things on earth, God will then bind them in heaven.

If that were the case, we'd be giving God orders and instructing Him. As Wagner points out, the crucial sequence is heaven first, *then* earth. We can only bind here what has already been bound in heaven.

Christ has already defeated Satan. We simply enforce what He has accomplished. In fact, all of our prayers are based on His finished work at Calvary.

How can we know what's been bound in heaven?

Contact

First, our constant contact with heaven is crucial. By maintaining a personal relationship with God through prayer, we know that if He chooses to reveal it to us, we will receive it. He sometimes speaks to us through Scripture—a certain passage may jump out as we're reading. For instance, it may be something that directly relates to the issue at hand. Or it may be something that the Holy Spirit applies specifically to our situation.

Discernment

We can also learn what's been bound in heaven from other believers, especially those with gifts of discernment. This is one reason team ministry is so important. Before Jesus departed earth, He sent His disciples out to confront the demonic in pairs (see Luke 10). As a pastor, I learned to be very aware of which church members were gifted with discernment. Frankly, I leaned on them from time to time.

Those with gifts of discernment or prophecy tend to be the most sensitive to what the Father is saying. They're like reconnaissance forces that hear and report our next assignment. I would ask my intercessors to write down and submit to me what they sensed God was saying about certain issues.

Knowing that even the best among us "see through a glass, darkly" and "prophesy in part" (1 Corinthians 13:9–12 KJV), I'd file these "words" in a notebook. I was especially interested in cases where two or three of them turned in words that seemed to relate. Scripture encourages us to let things be established by two or three witnesses (e.g., see Matthew 18:16). And over time, I learned which people were the most accurate. The body of Christ is amazing!

Often the directive to bind or loose will come in the regular flow of ministry. We may not have any revelation or guidance concerning a warfare issue until we become actively engaged with it. Here, it's in the battle's heat that God gives the assignment, and this is especially true in deliverance ministry, whether it's the deliverance of a person or a city or a nation.

SOME ADVICE ABOUT "TEARING DOWN"

Perhaps the biggest warfare mistake I see, currently, is the idea that we must somehow pull down every ruling spirit over our cities if we are to see revival. That seems to be the ultimate goal of many who call themselves spiritual warriors or warfare intercessors.

May I remind you:

> When a corrupting spirit is expelled from someone, it drifts along through the desert looking for an oasis, some unsuspecting soul it can bedevil. When it doesn't find anyone, it says, "I'll go back to my old haunt." On return, it finds the person swept and dusted, but vacant. It then runs out and rounds up seven other spirits dirtier than itself and they all move in, whooping it up. That person ends up far worse than if he'd never gotten cleaned up in the first place. (Luke 11:24–26 THE MESSAGE)

The purpose isn't simply to rid the heavenlies of wicked rulers. From this passage we learn that were the territorial spirits above our cities to be so weakened that they would withdraw, they then would wander in the dry places and return later with others seven times worse than themselves. In the end, our cities would be worse than in the beginning. That's *not* what we want.

Oh no. The purpose of spiritual warfare is *kingdom displacement*. I can empty the milk from a glass in two ways: Either I can pour out the milk or I can pour so much water into the glass that the water eventually displaces the milk.

I think we all know what would happen if Wal-Mart decided to build a mega-store in my mythical town of Tiny, Texas. Most likely within the first year or two, most of the mom-and-pop shops would be forced out of business.

But consider this: *Wal-Mart wouldn't have to tear down all of those little stores in order to build their supercenter.* All they would need to remove would be the two or three small stores that currently stood on the very site where the big superstore eventually would stand. The other shops in the area will soon disappear due to the success of the supercenter—*no "tearing down" needed.*

Here's my point: It's not a matter of our cleansing the heavenlies above our cities. It's a matter of our removing (by the Father's direction) those specific structures of darkness that are hindering the light of the gospel and thus the establishment of God's kingdom. When we seek first the kingdom, the other things also will be given to us (see Matthew 6:25–34).

Nevertheless, at times there *are* territorial princes that must be pulled down. God will make those assignments as He wills. God's kingdom will displace Satan's kingdom.

* * *

There are 1,200 to 1,500 demolition companies worldwide that raze skyscrapers, chimneys, towers, bridges, and other structures. At least two things set Baltimore, Maryland-based Controlled Demolition, Inc. (CDI) apart.

First, CDI, founded in 1960 by Jack Loizeaux (retired in 1984), today is a family business run by his two sons, Marc and Doug, and Marc's daughter Stacey.

Second, CDI is the globe's undisputed champion of large-structure implosions. Whether a 2,000-ton skyscraper, a 384-foot communications tower, or the Seattle Kingdome—by volume the largest building ever demolished by explosives—they will bring it down. CDI holds four Guinness Book world records and has imploded more than 7,000 structures—more than all of their competitors combined!

Their projects are amazing to witness. In mere seconds massive edifices crumble in on themselves in a shower of dust and debris. Perhaps the very essence of Controlled Demolition's work is in their name: CONTROL.

Each project CDI accepts requires months of precise planning by a world-renowned team of engineering experts to determine the best equipment, materials, manpower, and methods. Their goal? To guarantee complete predictability.

While being interviewed for a Learning Channel television special on CDI, President Marc Loizeaux was asked, "How do you determine how much explosive will be required to bring down a large structure?" Marc replied, "The secret isn't in knowing how much explosive to use; the secret is in knowing where to place it."

Engineers determine exactly which steel beam must be severed with explosives, what concrete masses must be pulverized, and in what sequence everything should happen. The building is then rigged with timed explosives. On the day of the implosion, one pressed button releases a chain reaction of explosions; the structure that required years to build collapses in seconds.

One day when I returned home from a speaking engagement, I was stunned to see that the beautiful four-bedroom home at the end of our block had burned to the ground. As I stood looking at the charred remains, the Lord spoke to my heart. He pointed out that while more than nine months went in to building the house, it was destroyed in less than ninety minutes.

Then he said, "Satan is angry about what the church is learning today about strategic prayer. He is angry because he has but a short time" (see Revelation 12:12). It has taken Satan thousands of years to construct his demonic network for promoting evil around the world. *What targeted strategic prayer can destroy in a few minutes, Satan has neither time nor resources left to rebuild.*[4]

INSIGHTS TO REMEMBER

- God put you here to give Satan headaches. You are dangerous.

- The power of attorney that Jesus gave us to use His name isn't carte-blanche authority. We're not to use His name as if it were a magic wand.

- God didn't put us here to merely survive. We are overcoming super-conquerors through Christ!

- Don't be frantically looking to find a demon-free zone. God prepares a table in the presence of your enemies.

- Any home where Christ is honored will have an occasional demonic *visitation*. What you don't want is for it to become a demonic *habitation*.

- It's about cleansing our homes to make them comfortable dwellings for the Holy Spirit.

- The right person at the right time—that is, in God's timing—can bind a demon. But we do not have the authority to bind other people.

- We will never have the power to bind or loose anything without the authority to do so.

- God is synchronizing heaven and earth.

- Christ has already defeated Satan. We simply enforce what He has accomplished.

- Whatever we bind or loose, in a spiritual sense, must have already been bound or loosed in heaven, else there will be no success.

- The purpose of spiritual warfare is kingdom displacement.

- Displacement is related to removing—by the Father's direction—those specific structures of darkness that are hindering the light of the gospel and thus the establishment of His kingdom.

- Satan doesn't have enough time left to undo the "damage" that the church can inflict on his kingdom through successful warfare prayer.

CHAPTER 10

THE AUTHORITY AND THE ANOINTING

Some Christians believe that because we're saved, we have "all authority." The truth is we don't; Christ does.

To this, they'd be quick to respond: "Yes, Christ does . . . and He lives in me, so I do too!"

And that's partly true. However, *authority has to do with assignment.*

You'll no doubt remember how Jesus gave spiritual "authority . . . to overcome all the power of the enemy" to the seventy before sending them out to confront demons (Luke 10:19). But the authority He gave them was for that assignment. Our authority is based on *our* assignment. Spiritual authority appears to be built into our lives in layers:

- *The new birth.* A measure of authority is given to us when we're born again—at least defensive authority to withstand the enemy's attacks.

- *Earned authority.* As we've observed, David first killed bears and lions. From there he graduated to "giant killer." Eventually he took cities and ultimately conquered kingdoms. Like David, we grow into levels of authority as we confront and defeat our enemies at different levels. "New levels, new devils."

- *Spiritual maturity.* A new believer can be spirit-filled, but spiritual maturity is a different matter. That maturity is developed over a period of years spent overcoming the enemy and experiencing life's trials through skillful use of the Word. With this comes a degree of spiritual authority.

- *Appointment.* There are certain tasks God will give us; tasks that will bring us face-to-face with powers of darkness. For these assignments, He gives us additional degrees of authority with which to overcome the enemy.

Regarding this last "layer," I can think of no better example than that of my own father.

When my father joined the U.S. Navy in 1943, he wasn't sent to boot camp. He also didn't begin as a seaman (the lowest rank) like I did years later. Dad joined at the height of World War II. He was a successful accountant, but the Navy needed him immediately at their base in Pensacola, so he went from the recruiting station in Birmingham directly to the Naval Air Station in Florida.

He walked onto the base, went to the disbursing office, and handed over his enlistment papers. They took him to the PX and bought him clothing and badges for a chief petty officer! He was immediately assigned duties according to that rank; he was given authority to operate at that level. When he was discharged, he was discharged as a chief petty officer. I was discharged a lowly seaman. Go figure.

Spiritual authority isn't unlike the badges, bars, and ribbons pinned on decorated war heroes. Unseen to us perhaps, but believe me, the enemy sees them and cringes when a spiritually mature, Spirit-filled veteran of much spiritual warfare walks into the room.

At any point, however, the Lord can and often does reinforce our authority with a greater measure than we normally carry, when we're facing new spiritual challenges and assignments. No demon is any match for the newest believer who's walking by faith, sold out to God, totally dependent upon Him.

CORPORATE ANOINTING

An internationally known Asian faith healer conducted a crusade in a Houston-area church several years ago. I attended a service and appreciated the integrity with which he ministered. For the first week, although many were prayed for, and though there were reports of many who'd been healed (some quite significantly), the evangelist wouldn't allow anyone to give public testimony of their healing. He insisted that they return with their doctor's report of their healing, complete with X-rays if possible, and a physician's letter verifying the healing. It wasn't until the second week that testimonies of healing and presentations of medical proof were allowed. Hundreds stood in long lines to share evidence.

One morning at our city pastors' prayer breakfast, this healing evangelist was our guest speaker. At the end of the breakfast I asked if I might speak with him privately. He graciously agreed, and I explained to him that I live in continual back pain. I asked if he'd take a moment and pray for my healing.

His answer surprised me.

Eddie, certainly I will pray for you. But before I do, I feel I owe you an explanation of how the gift of healing works through my life. I am not a healer. Jesus Christ, our Lord, is the healer. I'm simply a conduit through which His healing reaches the people. Furthermore, I wouldn't think that my prayer for your healing here, and now, would mean any more than if any of these other brothers were to pray for you. You see, when I am in the pulpit, surrounded by the body of Christ, I preach faith-building messages. As I do, the level of corporate faith begins to rise in the room. When *their* faith reaches a certain level, the Holy Spirit begins to heal the people. So it isn't me, or my faith; the Holy Spirit heals the people based on their faith.

Then he graciously and sincerely prayed for my healing. I wasn't healed, but I was genuinely touched by his honesty and transparency. We need more men and women like him.

What this man was explaining is that his authority to heal isn't "resident on or in him." It's given to him one assignment at a time. And it relates to the present level of corporate, shared faith.

You may have heard someone make a statement like, "Well, if he can heal the sick in his crusade, why doesn't he just go empty out the local hospital?" The reason is that although at times, and with some people, God does heal through this man's surrendered life, *it is God who heals.* And he doesn't direct or instruct God about whom to heal. God directs him—then empowers him. When somebody is healed, he's as surprised as anyone!

* * *

Alice and I were in a revival meeting at First Baptist Church in a small north Texas town. It was the last night, at the end of the service, and before the pastor dismissed the people I asked if I could say a word. I intended to thank them for their hospitality and say good-bye. However, when he handed me the microphone, the Lord's Spirit engulfed me.

How do I know? That's a good question. It was palpable; I could feel Him. The only way I can explain this is by likening it to the feeling you get when you walk through a pitch-dark place and hear an unexpected sound. Some describe it as "every hair on your body stands at attention." That's like the physical sensation I experienced, except that in the illustration about darkness, the sensation is accompanied by fear and evil. In the Spirit's case, it was accompanied by awe and reverence.

I was so concerned that I would grieve the Lord. I looked down at the pastor and the evangelist, sitting in the front row, and said, "Brothers, the Spirit of the Lord is on me." In unison they immediately replied, "Obey Him."

I waited patiently and silently for a couple of minutes until I sensed an instruction. Then I said, "The Lord is calling us to repent of our sin. If the Lord is convicting you of sin, stand and confess it now."

The Holy Spirit prompted people to confess their sins and be cleansed. Weeping broke out across the congregation. One after another they humbly stood and repented. The Lord was pleased and the Spirit's presence (the anointing) increased.

After some time—around eleven PM—a teenage girl leapt to her feet, threw her hands in the air, and screamed, "I'm a witch! Somebody, please help me!"

As she came to the altar, Alice and the pastor took her to his office for deliverance. The congregation and I prayed for victory until the door opened and the three of them returned.

The girl now had a peaceful presence about her. She smiled broadly and her cheeks were wet with joyful tears. She explained that her mother and father were deeply into witchcraft and had moved from a northern state after being charged with unlawful, unlicensed counseling.

She was born again and set free that night. What was the key? *The presence of the Holy Spirit in a corporate setting was so strong that darkness couldn't remain hidden.* That revival service didn't end until one in the morning. The church was transformed.

So at any point, the Lord can and often does reinforce our spiritual authority with a greater measure than we've known before, certainly greater than we normally walk in. This usually happens when we encounter new spiritual challenges and assignments, and when there is a corporate anointing.

Recall, too, that spiritual authority isn't as much about our *passion* as it is about His *purpose*. And it's definitely not a matter of volume. Some folks get louder and louder as they engage the enemy. This may be a result of their personality, or it may be a measure of their anger against darkness. There's certainly nothing wrong with this, but I assure you, demons are not deaf. If you're one of God's quieter kids, an anointed whisper of the right words at the right time can wreak havoc in the camp of darkness, so don't be intimidated by others. My point is: *Be authentic.* Volume isn't important; righteous obedience is!

There's a corporate anointing that's limited to an issue or to a moment in time. There's also a corporate anointing that rests upon a group, a ministry, or a congregation for an extended season.

In the 1990s, for example, Alice and I were pastors of a wonderful congregation in Houston. We were blessed with a unique anointing to pray for and see breakthroughs in our city and in our families. We also experienced what was to us a high level of anointing on our prayer journeys to the nations. This season of favor was about a corporate anointing over a church.

YOU AND I HAVE NO POWER

I have no power. You don't either. That's what Jesus essentially said:

> I'm telling you this straight. The Son can't independently do a thing, only what he sees the Father doing. What the Father does, the Son does. . . .
> I can't do a solitary thing on my own: I listen, then I decide. You can trust my decision because I'm not out to get my own way but only to carry out orders. (John 5:19, 30 THE MESSAGE)

These are the words the apostle John heard his Master say. Don't you imagine that they mystified him? After all, he'd seen Jesus do so many miraculous things. Nevertheless, if it's true of Jesus, it's also true of John, of you, and of me. I can clearly say and know, without hedging, that *in and of myself I possess no spiritual power.*

"I do nothing on my own, and I do only what I see God doing" (paraphrase). The inference is that the only power (anointing) available to us is that which relates to what the Father is presently doing. Why do I keep coming back to this? Because anything we attempt to do that the Father isn't actively doing, will be certainly powerless and potentially dangerous!

Perhaps this explains why often we see so little spiritual power in our lives and in our churches. We tend to focus on the task at hand rather than discern and discover what the Father is doing (if anything) about it. When we live this way, we may look impressive to some people, but what we do won't possess God's power.

* * *

One night I went to an altar for prayer. The presiding minister was moving among us, laying his hand on our foreheads, praying for us. (So far, so good.) When he came to me, he laid his hand lightly on my forehead and began to pray sincerely for me. After several minutes, though, in view of several thousand others, he seemed to become frustrated. As he did, he pressed my forehead more firmly, then more forcefully, actually pushing me downward.

At that point I opened my eyes and said quietly, "Sir, I'm not going to fall down to make you look good." With that, he moved on to the next person in line. His purpose was fine but his method was flawed.

There truly *are* times when the Holy Spirit rests so powerfully upon a person that standing is no longer a high priority. Some call this phenomenon being "slain in the Spirit." Actually, I think Ananias and his wife, Sapphira, were *slain* in the Spirit; or at least they were slain *by* the Spirit, when they lied about their property sale (see Acts 5).

I prefer instead to call this experience "*resting* in the Spirit." Do some people fake it? Definitely. Is it possible that some of it is merely psychosomatic (soulish)? Of course. But these don't negate it—there are pretenders in all corners of the church. That "fool's gold" (iron pyrite) only looks like real gold doesn't negate the existence of real gold.

* * *

An elderly evangelical minister visited our services one evening. An anointed guest evangelist prayed a powerful prayer over a group of people at the altar, the Spirit of God breathed on them, and many simply collapsed where they were. The service ended quietly as the Spirit continued to brood over those precious folks.

The visiting minister had never seen such a thing. I'm sure he'd heard of it, but he'd never witnessed it firsthand. He looked quite uncomfortable; his arms were crossed and his legs were crossed. He had a nervous expression on his face as I slid into the seat beside him.

"Are you all right, Pastor?" I asked.

"Yes," he said sternly.

"Is something bothering you?"

"No."

"Something is bothering you—what is it?"

He leaned over, pointed to a woman who was lying on the floor beside his chair and asked, "Who's going to minister to her?"

"He's doing it right now," I explained.

He rolled his eyes in disbelief. "And who would *he* be?"

"The Holy Spirit; He's ministering to her."

He only looked more perturbed.

"Would you like to know what the Spirit is doing?"

"Yes, I'd like to know."

I moved over and asked the woman if she could tell me what the Lord was doing. Without even opening her eyes she said yes.

Then I motioned for the pastor to come over so he could hear the explanation. He resisted at first but finally complied.

With him kneeling on one side of her and me on the other, she explained,

When I was three and four years old, my father's brother,

my uncle, would visit our family from time to time. I used to dread it. When the family was asleep he would come into my room and sexually assault me. Because of this, I've built walls around my heart so that no man could ever hurt me again.

I didn't know how to relate to my father. I've not known how to relate properly to my husband or my pastors. I've never gotten along with any male boss I've had. And now that my two sons are growing into manhood, I'm not relating properly to them.

But as I've been lying here on the floor, the Holy Spirit has been breaking down those walls I've built.

Her eyes were still closed, and a peaceful smile decorated her face as tears cascaded down her cheeks. "God is setting me free."

I looked at the elderly minister beside me. Tears were pouring down his cheeks as well. He leaned forward, gave her a fatherly pat on the shoulder, and said, "Sweetheart, just let the Lord finish what He's doing."

You see, this pastor was against what was happening because previously he'd only seen flawed methods. Until then he'd never recognized the true ministry of the Holy Spirit.

THE TRUE ANOINTING

It's said that a young Cassius Clay, the world heavyweight boxing champ, was seated on an airplane awaiting takeoff. A passing flight attendant said to him, "Sir, fasten your seat belt, please."

Clay, with his usual bravado, answered, "Ma'am, *Superman* don't need no seat belt."

To which the witty attendant said, "Sir, *Superman* don't need no *airplane*."

Good news: God isn't looking for Supermen or Superwomen. He works through folks like you and me. He's looking for recruits who will attend His boot camp and learn the art of warfare and then fight for victory.

* * *

A few years back a well-known televangelist came to town to minister to about twelve hundred faithful supporters. He's a dear friend, and his office called to invite Alice and me to attend. We accepted, and when we arrived we were ushered to the front row.

That night he was teaching on deliverance, and when he was done he said to the crowd, "In a moment I'm going to pray over you. As I pray, if you feel something inside you responding or reacting to my prayer, I want you to come to the altar for ministry."

He asked God to expose darkness and reveal the truth. By the time he'd finished, the altar was packed with people, some in full-blown demonic manifestation.

Two women in particular were wildly out of control. The evangelist noticed us in the front row and asked if we'd assist with them. They were too much for his security staff to handle.

I went to the one on his left, an East Indian woman. I commanded the demons in her to settle down and began to come against them in Jesus' name, commanding them to leave. (You'll find references to resources for this type of deliverance ministry in the back of this book.) Soon I had them under control. Before long the Lord revealed the name of the demonic strongman to me, and soon he and his "house" (the demons that he ruled) were cast out.

Then the woman saw my name tag and gasped. "Oh, I can't believe it's you, Pastor Eddie. Do you know who I am?"

When I apologized for not recognizing her, she told me. "Three weeks ago I called your office about my need for deliverance from demons. You prayed for me over the phone and cast out several demons that had been there as long as I can remember. You told me there might be more breakthrough coming. Tonight God brought you and me together to finish the job!"

I had to admit it was amazing that the two of us, in a city of more than four million people, would end up on the same night, at the same hotel, in the same ballroom, at the same altar! Hardly a coincidence.

Meanwhile, the evangelist was dealing with a young African woman who was so demonically strong that she was throwing two-hundred-plus-pound security men to the floor. The demons had her in their grasp, and when the evangelist challenged them, one screamed at him with a manly voice, "She's ours, you can't have her. We've had her for a hundred years!"

Again, he tried publicly to dislodge them, to no avail. Then, realizing they were hindering him from ministering to hundreds of others, he asked Alice and me if we would take her to an adjoining room to continue.

His security officers bodily carried her away and into a private area. All the while she was screaming and thrashing about, trying to smash her head against the concrete floor.

When she was finally in a private place and under control, Alice asked what seemed at the moment, an odd question: "Do you want to be free?"

The woman returned to her senses and said, "Oh yes. I found

out I had this demonic problem four years ago. And for the past four years I have looked for an anointed minister, evangelist, pastor, or church that could set me free." Yet all the while she continued to writhe and thrash about, wild-eyed.

I said, "Young lady, there is no anointed minister, evangelist, pastor, or church that can set you free. Your freedom was accomplished two thousand years ago when Christ died for your sins and shed His blood on Calvary."

Pausing to take in that truth, she breathed a long sigh of relief and sat up, in her right mind, delivered and celebrating Jesus!

So much so that when her mother saw her a few moments later she was shocked at even the look on her daughter's face. The next night she gave testimony of her deliverance.

Let's analyze what happened. The evangelist had attempted to cast the demons out of her. He was certainly right to try that. Alice and I often resort to casting out demons—this is what's called "a power encounter" (see chapter 5). However, Alice and I, not having to worry about ministering to 1,199 others in the room, led her into a truth encounter.

Why do you suppose God did this? Well, do you recall the object of her faith? She was looking for *an anointed man or ministry* to set her free. The evangelist couldn't have known it, but that's why he'd been ineffective. Although he is in fact an anointed man, God wasn't going to allow him to be *that* anointed man.

The Lord will not share His glory with us. That woman, set free in the way she had intended, would have seen not Jesus Christ but the evangelist as her deliverer. It was when she placed her faith in the finished work of the cross that she experienced her freedom. Again, too, remember that most deliverance ministry involves both truth and power encounters.

Nehemiah and his workmen rebuilt the walls of Jerusalem with a trowel (with which to lay the bricks and mortar) in one hand and a sword (with which to fight off the enemy) in the other. The walls represent truth; as long as the demonized person believes lies, the enemy can and will keep her bound. In deliverance ministry we use the "truth-trowel of the Spirit" to rebuild the walls of protection. At the same time, we wield the sword to evict any unclean spirits that have attached to or infiltrated her life.

The anointing is total dependency upon Christ. It's the refusal to trust anything or anyone but Him. It's not our strength that God requires but rather our weakness. We should never forget that the battle is the Lord's!

> His strength is made perfect—is manifested, is demonstrated in power—through our weakness. (See 2 Corinthians 12:7–10.)

To the degree that we are independent and self-sufficient, to that degree we are spiritually defeated and incapable of true spirit-empowered ministry.

ASSIGNMENT BEGETS AUTHORITY

On this particular trip, it was my last day in Lahore, Pakistan. What a wonderful time I'd had. For me to teach there, the government had insisted that hand-grenade screens be welded to the church's windows. Security was ordered to hand-wand (with a metal detector) everyone who entered the building. Twelve armed Muslim Pakistani soldiers stood watch around the perimeter. Two men with shotguns were stationed at the door.

God's Pakistani people are so hungry for Him. They had sat

almost motionless for three days as I taught. They didn't want to take a break, even for lunch. They wanted more of God's Word and wisdom.

That night I opened the service for altar ministry. "Come to the front, as you feel led, and I'll pray for you and share any insight I sense the Lord may give me concerning you."

It seemed like the entire congregation, mostly pastors and leaders and their wives, had moved toward the front for personal ministry. I knew it would take a long time, but that didn't matter to me, and it mattered even less to them.

I was about two-thirds finished when the back door burst open and a young man in his mid-twenties entered. He came down the aisle and offered himself to me for ministry. As I laid my hand on his shoulder and began to pray, he suddenly began to manifest a demonic presence, shouting loudly in Urdu, *to me,* "I worship you! I worship you!"

Of course I attempted to take authority over the demonic spirit. As I did, the man ripped his shirt open, popping off all the buttons, and began tearing it into shreds. He tore one piece off and fell to the floor, where he began cleaning my shoes.

It was clear I didn't have authority to deal with him at this time. So I asked my host to have two men escort him to the back of the auditorium. You see, I discerned that God hadn't sent him to me for deliverance. The enemy had sent him there to distract me from my true mission, to minister to those wonderful pastors and their wives.

I'd no sooner started when the demonized man began throwing the two men to the floor. Then he picked up a chair and slung it through a glass window.

Seeing the problem the men were having with him, I started toward the back of the room. My interpreter grabbed me by the arm and warned, "Don't go back there. You might get hurt. It isn't safe."

I explained, "This is not a matter of power. It's a matter of authority."

With that he released my arm, and I made my way back to intervene. I first instructed the men to release him. They did, although they were somewhat puzzled by the request.

The demons in him were focused on me. I didn't say another word. With my index finger I summoned him to come with me. Then I turned around, not looking back, and walked outside the building. He followed me quietly. Once outside on the lawn, I motioned for him to sit down on the grass and stay there. He did. (No matter what country, or what language is spoken there, I've never been anywhere that demons didn't clearly understand every instruction.)

I returned to finish my ministry. There was glorious victory that night. Later, when we exited the building, the demonized man was still seated obediently on the lawn.

I had been authorized—and therefore empowered (anointed)— to minister to the pastors and the wives. *That* was my assignment.

I also was authorized to lead the young man outside and to incapacitate the demons in him from doing further damage or causing further distraction. But I was not given authority to set him free. I prayed for him, but I realized that the rest will be someone else's job.

We need to drop the idea that we are to correct every person, meet every need, and solve every problem. That is not what God expects of us. The hardest word for many of us to say is a tiny two-letter word *no*. *Our job is to hear and obey God.*

For instance, every day I am swamped with prayer requests

from around the world. It's essential that I hear from God which, if any, I am to accept.

Perhaps the greatest example I can recall was at the end of an evangelistic service when a young twenty-something woman stopped me at the exit. She tearfully asked if I would counsel her. I told her I was sorry but that I couldn't. She tried to persuade me, but I held my ground.

Another person, overhearing her plea, chastised me. "I can't believe you aren't going to counsel her. She needs help."

I explained that I didn't sense God telling me that it was my assignment.

The next night, at the end of the evangelistic service, the young woman who had sought my counsel came down the aisle to confess her faith in Christ as her Savior. As she testified, she said,

> Last night I was under conviction and so miserable. As I was leaving, I asked Brother Eddie if he would counsel me. He refused.
>
> I drove home, went into my bedroom and fell across my bed. In desperation I cried, "Lord, I'm on my way to hell, and even the evangelist doesn't care. Save me, Lord!" And He did!

Then she turned and looked to me on the stage and said, with a tearful smile, "Thank you for not counseling me last night. I don't think I was desperate enough until I got home."

INSIGHTS TO REMEMBER

- Our authority is based on our assignment (see chapter 11).
- Spiritual authority, though unseen to us, causes the enemy to cringe in fear.

- The authority to heal isn't resident ("always accessible") in a person.

- Spiritual authority isn't about passion or volume. It's about purpose.

- Jesus said there's nothing He does on His own.

- We need to focus on what the Father is doing.

- Some believers aren't so much against spiritual *manifestations* as they are against certain spiritual *methods*.

- To the degree that a person places faith in a minister to help him, to that degree the minister can't. Our faith must be in God.

- To the degree that we're independent and self-sufficient, to that degree we're spiritually defeated and incapable of spirit-empowered ministry.

- We need to drop the idea that it's our job to correct every person, meet every need, and solve every problem.

- The hardest word for many of us to say is the tiny two-letter word *no*.

CHAPTER 11

THE ASSIGNMENT

My close friends know that I've never particularly liked the idea of WWJD ("What Would Jesus Do?"). Why? Because it assumes Christ's absence. I've always assumed His presence in my life!

"Who can tell me ten things the devil is doing in your city?" I asked an auditorium full of people at a spiritual warfare conference.

Almost every hand was raised, and several people jumped to their feet to offer an explanation of the enemy's activity.

To their surprise I said, "Never mind. Please return to your seats." After a moment I asked, "Who can tell me ten things *Jesus* is doing in your city?"

No one raised a hand. Most cocked their head to one side and stared quizzically. You'd have thought I was speaking Portuguese.

"If all of you know what the devil is doing, but none of you know what Christ is doing here, then how can you pray? Is what *Satan* does establishing the direction of your prayer?"

I'm convinced that 85 percent or more of our spiritual warfare praying is in response to something we perceive the devil is doing.

Why should this concern us? Because Jesus didn't react to Satan; He responded to the Father. Furthermore, it's *easier* to recognize and react to what the devil is doing than to wait upon the Lord and act only according to His revelation.

We are the bride of Christ. How can we even begin to help our Bridegroom do what He's doing if we don't know what that is?

WE ARE *NOT* GOD'S PROBLEM-SOLVERS

Many of us think that our assignment from the Lord is to identify problems and then apply prayer to them. We see ourselves as "God's problem-solvers," and we're works-oriented. To the contrary, that's not why we're here. We are here to do what we see the Father doing.

Oh, we know we're saved by grace through faith (see Ephesians 2:8–9). However, many of us feel we're saved *to work*! We think God saved us to serve Him. This isn't true any more than I married Alice so that she could serve me. We're saved to live in vital union, fellowship, and communion with Christ.

Failure to understand this will cause us to live lives of *spiritual drivenness*. We'll feel obligated to take any and every ministry or assignment that's offered. Why? Because we'll be mistakenly trying to establish our identity by what we do rather than by who we are. Some of God's most hard-charging servants have never had the sweet experience of falling asleep in the Father's lap. Some dread even appearing "spiritually unemployed."

* * *

For example, suppose there were a town called Tiny, Texas, and that it had ten churches. And imagine that First Church was the recipient of a bona fide revival. Praying people are excited to see genuine revival, so they would swarm First Church like fire ants at a picnic! Now, what would they pray once they got there? Quite simply, they'd pray for the other nine churches in town to experience the revival. Sounds good, doesn't it? But instead of partnering with God by acknowledging and celebrating Him for who He is and what He's doing, they are ignoring what He is doing at First Church and are trying to persuade God to send revival to the other nine churches. They're giving God instructions!

What would happen if they acknowledged God's current work? What if they became joint-venture partners with Him? What if they began to pray about what He was doing at First Church? Among other things, they could be *His* cheerleaders; God loves to be celebrated! God does what He does for praise, not out of pity.[1]

At the same time, they should ask the Lord for His direction and listen for His response. We need to both cheer Him *and* hear Him.

We prayer warriors are a passionate and aggressive type. That's good, to a point. But then our strength can become our weakness. Are we willing, with God's leadership, to wait? Or must we always be active?

A mature prayer warrior isn't afraid to wait and doesn't respond with a knee-jerk reaction to what the devil is doing. He or she stays in touch with "headquarters" and awaits instruction, knowing that one anointed word at the right time is worth more than hours of problem-centered prayer.

GIFTS AND CALLINGS

As a writer, I find words fascinating. They can move, bless, condemn, free, instruct, and even entertain people.

I've teased my grandchildren by pointing out that they're covered with *garments* (clothing); by telling them that their *epidermis* (skin) is showing; or by asking if they believe in *premarital intersexual digitation* (holding hands before marriage).

Now I must ask you: Have you *emulated* today? In prayer, as well as in any other aspect of our Christian walk, we should avoid "emulation" because according to Paul, it's a work of the flesh.

In the early '60s, I worked with a young pastor in California who was fascinated with evangelist Billy Graham. So much so that he preached with a North Carolinian accent. Not only that, but he dressed like Billy Graham, held his Bible like Billy Graham, and one day, when he showed me his sermon files, I realized they were Billy Graham's sermons (once produced like gospel tracts) that he would memorize and preach.

Certainly we should learn from our mentors. But we shouldn't emulate them. You will never please God trying to be like someone else. At the very least it's a form of envy, at its worst it's idolatry, and trying to be someone you are not calls into question God's creative wisdom.

Gifts

The Lord uniquely created you. He placed within you a spiritual gift that is your natural God-ordained motivation, and these gifts provide the foundation from which we operate. You'll find the list of motivational gifts in Romans 12:6–8, and the *King James Version* renders these as:

- Prophet
- Minister
- Teacher
- Exhorter
- Giver
- Ruler
- Mercy show-er

Each of these is every Christian's job. There are times all of us must hear and speak for Christ (prophet), meet the practical needs of others (minister), teach (teacher), give counsel and encourage others (exhorter), give (giver), organize and manage (rule), and empathize with and show mercy to others (mercy show-er). However, *one* of these is the *primary* motivating factor in your life.

Why is this important? Because the prayer of a person who shows mercy will be different from the prayer of a prophet. One who is a giver will pray differently than a teacher, and so on. The basic motivation of your life will directly affect how you pray and how you conduct spiritual warfare on any level.

Personalities

Beyond your spiritual gifting is your personality. In one method of categorizing personalities, there are four general types: radicals, progressives, conservatives, and traditionalists.

Radicals tend to be open, emotional, impulsive, and excitable. They often allow their emotions to elevate above their intellect.

Progressives are more staid and stable. They can be motivated to risk and venture into new areas; they also lean toward apathy and can slip into "paralysis by analysis."

Conservatives are mildly resistant to change, a bit guarded emotionally, and more passive than progressives. When it comes to change, they tend to feel obligated to protect the traditionalists.

Traditionalists, defenders of the status quo, are the most resistant to change. They tend to suppress their emotions and elevate their intellects.

Spiritual warfare intercessors, as you might know, tend to be more radical, emotional, and daring on the whole than many others.

Callings (Assignments)

Not only do we have individual gifts and individual personalities, we also have individual callings. Some are called to pray for nations. Others are called to pray for leaders. Still others are called to pray in times of crisis. And so on.

Surely you can see that with your motivational gift, your personality, and your divine calling, you dare not try to mimic your mentor. You *must* be yourself, the person God created you to be. Discover your gift, your personality, and your calling . . . and report for duty.

This will help you immensely when it comes to discerning your prayer and other ministry assignments. Out of thousands, Gideon selected three hundred. And while only those few had the assignment, all enjoyed the victory!

HEALING THE WOUNDED WARRIORS

Unfortunately, many would-be prayer warriors are still unqualified for battle. In fact, for them to engage in combat could endanger them or those close to them because they are wounded or compromised in some way.

Restitution

> If you enter your place of worship and, about to make an
> offering, you suddenly remember a grudge a friend has against
> you, abandon your offering, leave immediately, go to this
> friend and make things right. Then and only then, come back
> and work things out with God. (Matthew 5:23–24 THE
> MESSAGE)

Scripture clearly teaches that when we approach God, we first
need to be right with others. You've likely heard that you are to "owe
no man any thing" (Romans 13:8 KJV), a verse commonly used to
teach that it's wrong to borrow money. The *International Children's
Version* of this teaching, though, is succinct and illuminating: "Never
leave any bill unpaid." It's not wrong to borrow money as long as
you're current on the agreed payment schedule.

Some prayer warriors, however, have a trail of unpaid (and
never-intend-to-pay) bills in their past. They didn't repay their student loans; they've ignored traffic citations, parking tickets, income
tax payments, personal loans, and consumer credit delinquencies.
Some have filed bankruptcy simply because they can't stay out of the
malls. Some are so blind to their condition that they're asking God
to make Satan pay back seven times what he's stolen from them; all
the while God is making them pay back seven times what they've
stolen from others (see Proverbs 6:31).

In Malachi 3, we're taught that to fail to support the Lord's
work is to *rob* Him. If these things are true of us, we have a hole in
our armor and as yet are unqualified for battle.

Malachi also tells us that when we're faithful to support the
work of the Lord, He will rebuke the devourer on our behalf. I'd

give to the Father's work whether or not there's a financial reward, just to see Him rebuke the devil on my behalf!

If you need to make restitution, make a list of the issues. Immediately contact those you owe; apologize, work out a payment schedule you can live with, and keep to it. Then the Lord will begin to place you into battle-ready assignments.

Reconciliation

Some of us have broken relationships that need to be reconciled. I meet Christians, even those engaged in ministry, who haven't spoken to a parent, a sibling, or a friend in years because of a broken relationship.

God has told us we can't have a good relationship with Him unless we're consistently reconciling our relationships with others. We can't pray effectively for the lost to be saved and thus be reconciled to God when we aren't reconciled to one another. If you have a broken relationship, you have a hole in your armor. Make a list of those relationships and begin now to seek restoration.

Relationship With Jesus

Certain of the vagabond Jews, exorcists, took upon them to call over them which had evil spirits the name of the Lord Jesus, saying, We adjure you by Jesus whom Paul preacheth. And there were seven sons of one Sceva, a Jew, and chief of the priests, which did so. And the evil spirit answered and said, Jesus I know, and Paul I know; but who are ye? And the man in whom the evil spirit was leaped on them, and overcame them, and prevailed against them, so that they fled out of that house naked and wounded. (Acts 19:13–16 KJV)

I've had the privilege of leading several pastors, an evangelist, and a career missionary to saving faith in Christ. I can tell you this: Unless and until you know for certain that Jesus Christ lives in your heart, you are no match for the enemy. These seven sons of Sceva were beaten senseless by a demonized man. They may have been sincere, but they didn't know the Savior. Our relationship with Jesus is imperative to our victory over darkness.

To effectively combat the enemy, we must be certain he hasn't infiltrated our ranks. If demonic spirits have entered our lives, we will not be able to war effectively against them. It's essential that we fight from a strong and sure foundation.

Intimacy With God

Relatedly, to know the Lord as Creator God, transcendent, far-off, who is seated upon His throne, is good. But it's critical that we also know Him personally as our Father, present with us at the table. We will never have more authority against darkness than we have intimacy with Christ (see Revelation 3:20–21).[2]

Obedience

When Jesus was entered into Capernaum, there came unto him a centurion, beseeching him, and saying, Lord, my servant lieth at home sick of the palsy, grievously tormented.

And Jesus saith unto him, I will come and heal him.

The centurion answered and said, Lord, I am not worthy that thou shouldest come under my roof: but speak the word only, and my servant shall be healed. For I am a man under authority, having soldiers under me: and I say to this man,

Go, and he goeth; and to another, Come, and he cometh; and
to my servant, Do this, and he doeth it.

When Jesus heard it, he marvelled, and said to them that
followed, Verily I say unto you, I have not found so great faith,
no, not in Israel. (Matthew 8:5–10 KJV)

If we refuse to submit to authority, we will have no authority. It comes as a shock to some to learn that God's authority on
earth is dressed in a human being. Interesting, isn't it, how some
people claim to be ready, willing, and able to submit to God but
refuse to submit to His earthly authorities? There's no way around
it: Accountability involves human leadership. No one is simply
accountable to God. We also are accountable to one another.

Fruit of the Spirit

The Spirit's fruit (see Galatians 5:22–23) should be evident
in our lives. This fruit reveals that the Holy Spirit is in us and is
freely working through us. In us, and, therefore, through us, there
should be love, joy, peace, patience, kindness, goodness, faithful-
ness, gentleness, and self-control.

You see, the enemy has no fear of man. Nevertheless, he is terrified in the presence of the Lord. The fruit of the Spirit is living
proof of the Lord's presence.

God's Word

The Word of God is the only offensive weapon we possess. But
it's also the only weapon we need, because Satan's weapons are
nothing but falsehood and deception. Memorize and meditate on
God's written Word, and listen continually for His spoken word to

your heart. Scripture was what Jesus wielded against Satan in the wilderness following His forty-day fast (see Matthew 4).

The Blood of Christ

Did you know there's no biblical *instruction* to "plead the blood of Jesus," at any time, for any reason? Did you know there's no biblical *example* of "pleading the blood of Jesus," at any time, for any reason? Yet John does tell us that "they overcame [the devil] by the blood of the Lamb, and by the word of their testimony; and they loved not their lives unto the death" (Revelation 12:11 KJV).

The blood of Christ, which John tells us continually cleanses us from sin (see 1 John 1:9), and which Paul tells us makes God accessible to us (see Ephesians 2:13), *is* applied appropriately by the Lord. Biblical references to Jesus' blood refer primarily to its value; it was the awesome *price* God paid to redeem us. The only reference to His blood being *on someone* appears when, prior to the crucifixion, the frenzied crowd outside of Pilate's hall, shouted, "Let his blood be on us and our children!" (Matthew 27:25). In that case it was a symbol of judgment and condemnation, not of redemption.

All the same, I don't think we do a disservice to the Lord when we "plead the blood" over issues and individuals as we feel directed.

The Name

We have been given power of attorney; that is, we're given the right to pray to the Father "in the name of Jesus." It's important that we don't use Christ's name apart from His purposes.

For example, if I gave you power of attorney to sign in my name, I would be giving it to you for a specific purpose; a purpose for which, were I able, I myself would have signed. We don't only use His name, we *represent* His name, and that's far more serious. How do we know when to use it? By staying in constant contact with—abiding in—Him. (See John 15:7.)

Using our power of attorney is more than pronouncing the phrase, *in the name of Jesus.* Don't forget, the spirit world (where our enemy resides) is more revealing than the sensory world. A demon can easily recognize whether or not we're authentic, authorized, and anointed. Sure, we can easily say the words . . . but would a review of our lives show that we represent God? And, more important, are we using His name to do what He would do? *That's* how to use power of attorney.

PRAYER VERSUS PROCLAMATION

The following could well be the most significant information I'll share in this book.

Warfare Prayer

Spiritual warfare often involves prayers and/or proclamations. *Warfare prayer* is directed to God concerning the battle. When it comes to prayer, we can ask God for anything. We are His children.

I have four kids. They can ask me for *anything.* Some of what they request I'll provide. Other things, I won't. (I'm certainly glad the Father hasn't given me everything I've asked for in the past—if He had, my life today would be a wreck.) Nevertheless, my children can come to me with *whatever* is on their heart. And you and I can do the same with our Father God.

When I was a boy, my parents scolded me (or worse) for "tattling" on either of my two brothers. Tattling wasn't allowed.

Regarding spiritual warfare, though, I *encourage* tattling! For example, when our children where quite young (preschool), we taught them that whenever they felt like "something bad" was in their room (we didn't use terms like *demon* or *evil spirit* with them at that age), they should tell God—tattle to their Heavenly Daddy. We assured them that they could trust Him to deal with it appropriately.

One afternoon our son Bryan, in junior high at the time, returned from school and uncharacteristically brushed past me, moving briskly toward his room with his hand over his mouth. I followed him and asked if he was okay. He nodded, his hand still covering his mouth.

Upon further examination and investigation, though, I discovered that he'd been beaten up on the bus by Charlie, an older and larger student.

"What did you do to provoke Charlie?" I asked.

"Nothing, Dad."

"Son, you must have done something to anger him. No one would beat up someone else just for the fun of it."

"Charlie did," Bryan insisted.

I didn't say anything more; I just helped him clean up.

Later that night, after dinner, I got Bryan's attention. "Son, come with me. You and I are going to Charlie's house."

He was immediately fearful, but I said, "You don't need to worry—I'll do all the talking. Everything will be all right."

With that, we walked down the street. When I knocked on the door, Charlie's dad invited us in. "What's on your mind?" he offered.

"We came so that my son can apologize to your son." I said. I looked over at Bryan and saw that though he looked fully confused, he trusted me. I'd promised him he'd have no problem and that I'd take care of things.

"Charlie!" his dad yelled. "Come in here."

Charlie, seeing us as he walked in and sat down, was the most nervous of all.

"So what did Bryan do to Charlie? Why does he need to apologize?"

"We're not sure about that. In fact, we were hoping Charlie could explain. You see, Charlie beat up Bryan today on the way home from school. So I'm certain Bryan must have done something serious to deserve it."

"Charlie, did you beat Bryan up?" His dad asked.

Charlie grunted a nonverbal but obvious yes.

"What did he do to you that made you beat him up?" his dad pushed further.

Charlie shrugged his shoulders. "Nuttin'."

"He did nothing to you, and you beat him up?" With that, Charlie's dad took his son by the arm and led him to a back room, from which we heard "weeping, wailing, and gnashing of teeth."

When they returned, his dad said, "Charles, you apologize to Bryan for what you did."

"Sorry," was the fourteen-year-old equivalent of an apology.

Then I said, "Charlie, we certainly forgive you. However, be assured that if something like this ever happens again, we'll be back for a visit."

It never did happen again, and ironically Bryan and Charlie became good friends.

Just as my son was wise to trust his situation to me, it's wise for us to report the enemy's activity to the Father—for us to "tattle"—and ask Him to administer the correction.

Warfare Proclamations

Warfare proclamations are an entirely different issue. Unlike prayer, we don't have permission to say anything we want to the enemy. We are only ambassadors, and as such, we are only free to say to the enemy what our Head of State (Christ Jesus) tells us to say. Nothing less, and nothing more. Once again—and please remember this—*that* is our assignment.

INSIGHTS TO REMEMBER

- Don't let what Satan is doing establish the direction of your prayer.
- It's easier to react to satanic activity than to wait upon the Lord and act only according to His revelation.
- Too many Christians see themselves as "God's problem-solvers."
- Trying to be like someone else is at least envy and at worst idolatry.
- We should learn our motivational gifts; they will guide us toward God's directives for our lives.
- We would do well to accept our personality type. Be genuinely *you*!
- We need to know our calling.
- Until we've made Jesus our Lord and Savior, made restitution, and reconciled ourselves to others, we aren't in a position to war effectively.

- We will never have more authority against darkness than we have intimacy with Christ.

- Only those who submit to authority are given authority.

- Since the enemy has no fear of man, it's God's presence in our lives—evidenced by the Spirit's fruit—that terrifies him.

- God's Word, the sword of the Spirit, is our only offensive weapon.

- The blood of Jesus and the name of Jesus empower us against the enemy.

- With regard to warfare prayer, speaking to our Father, we can say anything and ask Him for anything.

- With regard to warfare proclamation, we are only to speak to the enemy what the Father is speaking.

CHAPTER 12

FINAL INSIGHTS

In my early years as an evangelist, I worked with a ventriloquist figure I called "Leroy." In one of my routines, when I took Leroy out of his suitcase, he was wearing a U.S. Army hat. I'll spare you the whole routine, but toward the end I asked, "Leroy, does the devil ever sneak up on your blind side and get the better of you?"

"Nope," he'd answer.

I'd ask why, and he'd answer, "Because I ain't got no blind side."

With that, I'd spin his head around 360 degrees; my crowd always laughed.

Real people, like you and me, *do* have blind sides. That's why we're instructed to "walk circumspectly" (that is, walk looking around—Ephesians 5:15-16).

DIVERSIONARY TACTICS

What do you do when you confront a demon? Or what would you do *if* you were to confront a demon? I sometimes ask people this, and I often hear something like, "Well, duh, I'd bind it, or rebuke it—of course!"

"Where does the Bible tell you to do that?" I ask.

Why do we have such a "knee-jerk" reaction to the enemy? For one thing, as a military concept, have you ever heard of "diversionary tactics"? Frequently, in warfare, to catch an enemy off balance, you'll create a diversion. Once he's focused on the diversion, you attack his blind side.

This is only one reason we should not get lured into determining our own targets and developing our own strategies. Be everdependent on the Holy Spirit, especially when you are confronted by forces of darkness.

* * *

Chapter 5 of our *Spiritual Housecleaning Workbook,*[1] called "Spiritual Church Cleaning," begins with the story of Alice and me, along with our team of intercessors, going into a small, spiritually dead church to determine the reason it had never grown.

We discovered that the church had lost their pastor in 1958, and had been so broken over the incident that they'd written into their minutes: "This past week, Jerry Jennings, our new young pastor, was killed in a tragic auto accident. When Pastor Jerry died, the vision of our church died with him." The minutes were approved and became part of their legal identity. Tragically, they had cursed themselves and didn't even know it.

That night the following occurred.

With our intercessors, we had just sat down to begin worship and prayer, when suddenly three of them gasped simultaneously and pointed to a spot just above the Lord's Supper table at the front of the auditorium.

"What do you see?" I asked.

The three intercessors explained that above the table, directly in front of me, stood a huge, ferocious-looking demon. I looked where they were pointing and said, "Go in peace."

They looked surprised and giggled.

"What happened?" I prodded.

They said that when I told the spirit to go in peace, he looked completely surprised—actually, relieved—and darted away.

They'd no sooner said this when one of the elders stood, Bible open, and began to read an Old Testament passage wherein a king that had been captured in war, contrary to logic was released to go in peace. The elder added, "This was part of my devotional reading this morning!"

I had acted almost instinctively to what I sensed the Spirit was saying. To us, this emphasis on that Scripture was confirmation that although it seemed illogical, I'd indeed done the right thing by allowing the demon to go free.

I shouldn't have to tell you that I'm no genius. When I'm ministering, I don't try to figure things out logically. I've found that if I engage spiritually with what I'm doing, and if I'm walking in God's favor, the Holy Spirit will be working with me, and, therefore, the first thing that comes to my mind, typically, is His direction.

While doing ministry, the one thing I keep in the forefront of my mind is what I've said repeatedly in this book: *Of myself I can do nothing, and I'm only to do what the Father is doing.* I'm here to work the works of Christ who sent me. I feel no pressure at all to perform or even to succeed. I simply relax in the knowledge that Christ in me is the hope of glory. I listen to what He's saying (in my heart) and watch what He's doing.

Like the one that appeared above the altar of that church, demons most often voluntarily appear for one reason: to distract us from focusing on the Lord. Why? Because demons know that our power over them is directly linked to our focus upon and attention to the Holy Spirit. If they capture our attention, we lose our power. Accordingly, when it comes to encounters with darkness—and believe me, I've had my share—I practice a no-knee-jerk response. Typically, unless redirected by the Lord, I ignore them, neither binding them nor rebuking them. Being ignored drives the enemy crazy.

Demons love to fight. They *live* to fight. Knowing that, why would we oblige them, except at the direction and in the power of our Commander in Chief?

* * *

I mentioned earlier that during my Navy days I served onboard a destroyer in the Pacific. Serving on that ship, at sea for weeks at a time, could feel somewhat like prison life.

There were a handful of sailors on our ship who were continually in and out of trouble. They were profane, stayed drunk when we were in port, and were consistently violent. It wasn't unusual to see one of them bloodied from some fight he'd provoked—laughing and already talking about his next bout. He simply loved to fight.

Knowing that a man can stoop to such a low existence, it's easy for me to grasp that a demonic spirit could express that same attitude. I refuse to fight them unless otherwise ordered. To them, more than any pain we might cause them, combat is little more than entertainment.

PROTECTION AND HEALTH

I often ask my audiences, "If God gives you a spiritual warfare assignment, will He protect you while you carry it out?" I typically get looks that seem to say, "Duh, of course. What a stupid question." Mostly people nod in agreement and say something like, "Yes. If God gives me an assignment, He'll protect me during and through it."

Then I ask my follow-up question: "In that case, what did Stephen do wrong? God gave him a spiritual warfare assignment, and he died while obeying" (see Acts 6–7).

We've been taught (by our teachers, not by God) that our protection and health are guaranteed by the Lord. Listen: If your protection and health are your highest consideration, you're reading the wrong book, and you're not prepared for spiritual warfare. It's your kingdom potential that's your most valuable possession. If you're not prepared to die for Christ, then you aren't really prepared to live for Him. Were God obligated to protect us, there would be no martyrs!

* * *

Many years ago, on a family vacation in Southern California, we visited the Orange County Fair. While there, our children found an amazing ride that seemed so utterly outlandish people were wagering on whether or not to get on it. Bryan, a sky diver, began challenging me, and frankly, I was ready to take the leap. Suddenly, though, the Lord said to me, "Take no unnecessary chances. I have plans for you." With that, I had to opt out of something I'd *really* have enjoyed doing.

Later, while reflecting on that experience, I asked the Lord why He refused to allow me to "take the risk."

He said, "Eddie, soldiers get killed in bars as well as in battle." I got it. As for me, I'd rather die in battle; and if I must die, I want the enemy to suffer in the process. I don't want to "die for nothing."

A few years back I had the privilege of meeting the director of an orphanage in India. She was a beautiful woman in her mid-forties who glowed with the presence of Jesus, one of the most vibrant, pleasant, gracious women of God I've ever met. At the time she was caring for seventy-four children in a mud house with a tin roof.

I would never have guessed that the reason she was Mother to all those orphans is that one day her young preacher husband went down the street for a few groceries. When he didn't return, she stepped outside to look for him. To her horror, she discovered his body, cut into seven pieces, lying in front of their home. Friend, we in America have little understanding of the price some people in other nations pay simply to love Jesus.

On my last trip to Pakistan, I sat down with my family and staff. I told them that God had given me a personal promise of protection the last time I went, but this time I'd not been given such an assurance. "If I should not survive this," I instructed, "don't say or allow it to be said: 'If he'd been here at home like he should have been, this would have never happened. But no—he had to play the big shot and go to a country that he knew full well wasn't safe.'" I don't know if anyone actually would have said that, but frankly it sounds a lot like what I sometimes hear from Christians. They put a higher premium on their well-being and safety than on their kingdom assignment.

Some of us will have to *live our lives* to reach our kingdom potential. Others of us will have to *give our lives* to reach our king-dom potential.

* * *

Where did we get the idea that protecting us is God's highest priority?

Such errors are typically a result of misunderstanding Scripture. When I ask people, they usually remind me that Jesus promised, "I give to you power . . . over all the power of the enemy, and *nothing shall by any means hurt you*" (Luke 10:19 KJV, emphasis mine). That indeed is what Christ said. But He wasn't saying it universally. He was speaking it to the disciples He was about to send out to confront demons without Him.

Remember: This was pre-Pentecost. These followers did not yet have the Holy Spirit's presence in their lives, for He had yet to be sent. They were no match for the smallest demon. Had Jesus not made special arrangements, these seventy witnesses that He was commissioning would have become "the *seventy* sons of Sceva" (see Acts 19)!

You see, Jesus knew He was going away. He knew He was leaving them behind. This assignment was essentially a training exercise. They needed a little on-the-job training. As with our military today, "war games," in which we pretend to fight each other, are intended to prepare us for the real thing, if and when it should come.

So Jesus promised the disciples that nothing would hurt them, and sure enough, they came back rejoicing, even gloating at having power over the demons and being unharmed. He said, in essence, "Don't be excited about your power over the enemy. I set that up for you. Be excited to know that your name is written in my book" (see Luke 10:20).

This story is often used to convince people of God's continual and automatic protection, especially when they're engaged in spiritual warfare. They might even believe they have immunity when fighting the devil. They think that while Satan and his army shoot blanks, we shoot real bullets. But they fail to realize that this "protection clause" only applied to this group, on this assignment. History records that many of these same seventy followers of Christ died merciless deaths for His sake. They were martyred for their faith. My point? Something eventually *did* hurt them.

Let's grow up and accept the fact that dying for Jesus may be our assignment as well. If so, we accept it for His sake. Warfare is about dedication and discipline: We must know when to be silent and when to fight, when to be passive and when to act. This is not a good day for spiritual know-it-alls. It's not a good time to move with partial revelation. How well-equipped are you? How sharp is your sword? How well do you know God's Word?

Additionally, we need the Lord's direction. Consider the following story from Alice's book *Forty Days Beyond the Veil*.[2]

OBEDIENCE

I [Alice] have always been a warrior. When I was a teenager, my friends nicknamed me Bulldog. Just as a bulldog will grab and hold the pant leg of its victim, I will take a prayer issue and hang on to it until I see something happen. However, untrained and undisciplined warriors can be a danger to themselves and to others—as I was during my earlier years.

In the 1980s, I began to research the history of the city in which we live. It soon became clear to me the nature of the spiritual darkness we were facing. My heart burned in prayer for Houston, America's fourth largest city. With the tenacity of a bulldog I sought the Lord, intent on finding out what territorial spirits held our city in their grip. Daily I begged the Lord for insight.

One winter morning during prayer, I felt the Lord speak to me about my city's spiritual condition. I sensed that He was telling me the names of the demonic princes that are the "puppet masters" assigned to carry out Satan's bidding. They rule in the affairs of men through wicked and deceived leaders.

Arrogantly (although I didn't realize it at the time), I began to bark at the principalities that hindered our city. From my prayer closet I zealously attacked them in fervent warfare. "In the name of Jesus, you spirit of _____, I command you to get out of Houston. We don't want you here. I stand against your every scheme to steal, kill, and destroy."

After several weeks of ranting and raving against these workers of darkness, their counterattack came against me like a nuclear blast. I came within ten hours of dying from peritonitis of the spleen and liver. That's not all. Eddie and I had six major surgeries in fourteen months, and three of them weren't covered by insurance. Our savings were depleted and we were on the brink of losing our home. With a growing family, a new baby, and a young church that had just lost its first pastor, I was in a terrible place. To the demons' delight, the church was struggling, our family was struggling, and I was struggling.

"And it came to pass," found 446 times in the Bible, is one of my favorite portions of Scripture! Thankfully, painful times do pass, and eventually the dust settled around us. I had believed that all of this persecution from the powers of darkness had come because I was such a godly person. Boy, was I wrong!

One morning, I was praying about all that we had experienced. The Lord spoke so clearly to my heart that I can almost hear the echo of His voice to this day. He said to me, "Alice, I told you the names of the spirits over Houston, but you never asked Me what you were to do with the revelation." I could hardly believe it! Now I know—diagnosis doesn't necessarily mean assignment! Knowing what is wrong, and being told to correct it, are two completely different issues.

Has Christ given us authority to deal with the enemy? Absolutely, He has! But the authority given to us is ambassadorial, not carte blanche. We are not called to be spiritual Rambos—an army of one. We are called to be disciplined warriors who explicitly follow the orders of our Commander in Chief and the Lord of Hosts—the Lord Jesus Christ. Our Lord's timing and assignment to the battle are critical. To engage the enemy without His direction is presumptuous at best. With the best of intentions, but with arrogance and pride, I found myself fighting for my life in a battle I had picked on my own. I repented to the Lord and then to Eddie. It was a costly lesson but one I will never forget.

My preacher husband often says, "We have two teachers in life: *mentors* and *mistakes*. We choose whether we will learn from our mistakes or from our mentors." I trust I am your mentor today. Please take this issue to heart and learn from this bulldog!

Now contrast that experience of Alice's with this one that I tell in my book *Intercessors*.[3]

One morning my wife, Alice, went shopping for building supplies for a project. Alice, being an intercessor and not a construction worker, was unfamiliar with the items and spent a considerable amount of time in the hardware store looking for them. Finally, Alice found the items and was standing in the checkout line when, suddenly, she had a brief vision. In her mind's eye—a closed vision—she saw a man standing in my office pointing a gun at me.

Immediately, she grabbed her purse, abandoned her shopping cart, and ran to the car. Alice began to intercede, even as she drove home. Once home, she rushed inside to her prayer closet, where she began crying out to the Lord.

Alice prayed for forty-five minutes until the burden and the sense of urgency subsided. Only then did she call the office and ask, "Eddie, are you OK?"

"Yeah, fine." I answered. "Why do you ask?"

She told me about her vision and how she had entered into prayer.

"Oh that," I explained. "He just got saved."

That morning I had had a counseling session with a medical doctor who was in ill health, separated from his wife, addicted to narcotics, and suicidal. After I led him to Christ—and through some significant deliverance—he explained how he had loaded a pistol that morning and placed it on his kitchen counter, intending to bring it to my office and first kill me, then himself. For some "unexplained reason," he absent-mindedly left the pistol on the kitchen counter.

Since then she has been asked, "Alice, why didn't you call the office and ask if he was all right?"

"It was time to pray, not take a survey," she replies.

Alice's ability to hear and obey God that day saved my life.

A SURPRISING REVELATION

It was a beautiful sight, our panoramic view from where we stood atop the mountain overlooking a small village in India. Alice and I were in the country to teach at a prayer conference and had taken the time away to visit the village. Now we had come up to the mountaintop to pray for it.

The village was filled with poverty and sicknesses of all sorts, including leprosy. As I began to pray, I was almost instantly and unexpectedly "clothed" with an intercessory anointing. My heart was broken, and I wept openly as I seemed aligned and joined with Christ regarding the village. I was experiencing His broken heart for its people.

(By the way, this "intercessory anointing," as I call it, is quite common to those whose primary ministry is prayer. But for me, it was quite a surprise.)

When I'd finished crying out for the souls of the villagers, I asked the Lord, "Father, what just happened to me?"

He said, to my heart, "You are *a territorial spirit.*"

(Before you think I've entirely lost my mind, keep reading. There really is a lesson to be learned here.)

My definition, and likely yours, of a territorial spirit is a prince demon who "oversees" a territory. So imagine my astonishment to hear the Lord tell me that *I* am one. Frankly, I didn't know what to do with it!

I've learned through the years that when you receive a mysterious word from the Lord, keep asking questions.

So, I prayed, "Lord, what do you mean, I'm a territorial spirit?"

There was no answer.

Again I asked, "Why did you call me *a territorial spirit,* Lord? Still nothing.

Do you know what? The way the Lord speaks to me really bothers me. He'll say something like, "Eddie?"

I'll say, "Yes Sir."

"Lift up your right foot and lean slightly to your right."

I'll do it, and then say, "Lord, now what?"

And He says, "Now, check back with me in about six months."

Six months! What do you mean, "check back" in six months! I want to know where I'm going, how I'm going to get there, and when I'll arrive.

And yet He offers me only the slightest information. If I didn't know better, I'd think He wants to keep me continually dependent upon Him! (smile)

You see, I'm an independent sort. The Father knows me well enough to keep me under rein. I feel like a horse with a bridle in its mouth—being steered by the Lord.

I received no answer that day, or the next. In fact, six months later, when I was sitting in my "prayer chair" (Alice has a prayer closet; I have a prayer chair), I said, "Lord, what did you mean that day when you told me I am a territorial spirit?"

I sensed Him say, "Look at 2 Corinthians, chapter 10."

I turned to it and began to read. I was shocked at what I discovered. Let me show it to you, along with, in brackets, the insight He gave me that day.

> We do not dare to classify or compare ourselves with some who commend themselves. When they measure themselves by themselves and compare themselves with themselves, they are not wise. [There is to be no competition in the body of Christ. Each of us has his own assignment.]
>
> We, however, will not boast *beyond* proper *limits* [*beyond* and *limits* are territorial words], but will confine our boasting to the *field* God has assigned to us, a *field* that *reaches* even to you [*field* and *reaches* are both territorial words].
>
> We are not *going* too *far* in our boasting, as would be the case if we had not *come* to you, for we did get as *far* as you with

the gospel of Christ [*coming* and *going,* and *near* and *far*—all territorial words].

Neither do we go *beyond* our *limits* by boasting of work done by others. Our hope is that, as your faith continues to grow, our *area of activity* among you will greatly expand [the term *area of activity* speaks of a territory], so that we can preach the gospel in the *regions beyond* you. [A region is a territory.] For we do not want to boast about work already done in another man's *territory.* (vv. 12–16, emphasis mine)

I *got* it! Paul's statement about "another man's territory" implies that each of us has been assigned a "field" or a territory. And we are spirit beings, clothed in human flesh—*territorial spirits.*

In addition, the plan is for our territories to "expand." It's up to God to expand them as we are fruitful in ministry. Paul tells the Corinthian Christians he hopes that as *they* continue to grow in faith, *his* "area of activity" will "greatly expand."

Frankly, I'm uncomfortable with the sound of this. And I'd suggest you not walk around referring to yourself as "a territorial spirit" in relating to other people, in general. But this revelation did bring a phenomenal truth across to me: I have a God-assigned territory. My anointing and authority is sufficient for the completion of my territorial assignment. The most important thing is for each of us to know our assignments and our assigned areas. It's our God-assignment, our personal territory, for which we will one day stand before Him and give account.

GOALS

We observed earlier that the purpose of all things is the same: to bring glory to God's name. Every one of us has personal goals for our lives, for our families, for our churches, for our cities, and for our world. I'll finish by saying that there are some primary overall (shared) goals as well. These include:

- That God's kingdom will come (Matthew 6:10)
- That God's name will be glorified (Matthew 6:9)
- That the earth will be filled with the knowledge of God's glory (Habakkuk 2:14)
- That God's house will be filled with children (Matthew 28:19–20)
- That we may live quiet and peaceful lives (1 Timothy 2:2).

INSIGHTS TO REMEMBER

- Depend on the Holy Spirit when confronted by forces of darkness.
- When ministering, engage spiritually, not logically.
- Demons know that our power over them is directly linked to our focus upon and attention to the Holy Spirit.
- If demons capture our attention, we lose our power.
- Demons love to fight. They live to fight. Ignoring them drives them crazy.
- Were God always obligated to protect us in battle, there would be no martyrs.
- Some are called to *live* our lives to reach their kingdom

potential. Others are called to *give* their lives to reach their kingdom potential.

- We must learn when to be silent and when to fight; when to be passive and when to act.
- This is not a good day for spiritual know-it-alls.
- We are territorial spirits.
- Our God-given assignments will involve our "territory."
- Our anointing and authority therein *will* be sufficient.

ENDNOTES

CHAPTER 1: THE GREATEST WAR

1. Adapted from *The Wall Street Journal,* as quoted in G.B.F. Hallock, *2500 Best Modern Illustrations* (New York: Harper & Brothers, 1935), 374.

2. David Ireland, *Journey to the Mountain of God: Pursuing Intimacy with Your Creator* (New York: Warner Faith, 2006), 247.

3. Rebecca Greenwood, *Authority to Tread* (Grand Rapids, MI: Chosen, 2005), 9.

CHAPTER 2: THE SATANIC STRATEGY

1. Morris Cerullo, *You Can Know How to Defeat Satan* (San Diego: Morris Cerullo World Evangelism, 2002), 77.

2. Charles Swindoll, *The Tale of the Tardy Oxcart* (Nashville: Word, 1998), 154.

CHAPTER 3: THE ENEMY'S TARGETS

1. Eddie Smith, *How to Be Heard in Heaven: Moving From Need-Driven to God-Centered Prayer* (Minneapolis: Bethany House, 2007).

2. Morris Cerullo, *Strategies of Satan* (San Diego: Morris Cerullo World Evangelism, 2000), Table of Contents.

CHAPTER 4: THE ORIGINAL DESIGN

1. Charles R. Swindoll, *The Tale of the Tardy Oxcart* (Nashville: Word, 1998), 147.

CHAPTER 5: THE GROUND-LEVEL BATTLEFIELD

1. At *www.prayerbookstore.com* Alice and I provide all-day seminars, individual teachings, and books to equip Christians for deliverance ministry.

2. Eddie Smith, *Breaking the Enemy's Grip* (Minneapolis: Bethany House, 2004).

3. Alice Smith, *Delivering the Captives:Understanding the Strongman— and How to Defeat Him* (Minneapolis: Bethany House, 2006). We also team-teach seminars on this subject; these are available in both CD and DVD formats. These resources likewise may be found at *www. prayerbookstore.com.*

4. Oswald Chambers, *My Utmost for His Highest* (New York: Dodd, Mead, and Company, 1935), 201, entry for July 19.

CHAPTER 6: THE OCCULT-LEVEL BATTLEFIELD

1. From Exodus 20:5, *King James Version*. Here God tells the Israelites that they are to worship Him only. He's jealous for their worship.

2. Trust me, that's not what He means. God's not jealous *of* Oprah or *of* anyone else.

3. See at *www.youtube.com/watch?v=NpPTxsdc5Hw&NR=1;* I also encourage you to see the clip at *www.youtube.com/watch?v=JW4LLwkgmqA &feature=related.*

4. In C. Peter Wagner, ed., *Breaking Strongholds in Your City: How to Use Spiritual Mapping to Make Your Prayers More Strategic, Effective and Targeted* (Ventura, CA: Regal, 1993), 85–86, in chapter 3, "Dealing With Strongholds."

5. Alice and Eddie Smith, *Spiritual Housecleaning: Protect Your Home and Family from Spiritual Pollution* (Ventura, CA: Regal, 2003).

6. Adapted from Eddie Smith, *Breaking the Enemy's Grip* (Minneapolis: Bethany House, 2004), 138–39.

7. This section is adapted from ibid., 139–41.

CHAPTER 7: THE TERRITORIAL-LEVEL BATTLEFIELD

1. I have written, recorded, and published many warfare songs. Warfare music certainly has a place in our repertoire. Allowing it to replace praise and worship isn't that place.

2. See *www.adherents.com/religions_by_adherents.html.*

3. This passage speaks of Sennacherib, wicked king of Assyria. However, it's also descriptive of God's judgment upon Satan's activity.

4. For instance, see *www.missionfrontiers.org/newslinks/statewe.htm.*

5. See *www.sentinelgroup.org/vsg2001.asp.*

6. C. Peter Wagner, *Praying With Power* (Ventura, CA: Regal, 1997), 75.

CHAPTER 9: THE REAL POWER

1. Adapted from Eddie and Alice Smith, *Intercessors and Pastors: The Emerging Partnership of Watchmen and Gatekeepers* (Houston: Spiri-Truth Publishing, 2000).

2. Alice and Eddie Smith, *Spiritual Housecleaning* (Ventura, CA: Regal, 2003) and *Spiritual Housecleaning Workbook* (Regal, 2007).

3. C. Peter Wagner, *Confronting the Powers* (Ventura, CA: Regal, 1997), 155.

4. This section is from Eddie Smith and Michael L. Hennen, *Strategic Prayer: Applying the Power of Targeted Prayer* (Minneapolis: Bethany House, 2007), 17–18.

CHAPTER 11: THE ASSIGNMENT

1. I address this more thoroughly in my book *How to Be Heard in Heaven* (Minneapolis: Bethany House, 2007), 99-100.

2. Take a look at Alice Smith's *Spiritual Intimacy With God: Moving Joyfully Into the Deeper Life* (Minneapolis: Bethany House, 2008), available at *www.prayerbookstore.com.*

CHAPTER 12: FINAL INSIGHTS

1. Alice and Eddie Smith, *Spiritual Housecleaning Workbook* (Ventura, CA: Regal, 2007).

2. Alice Smith, *Forty Days Beyond the Veil* (Ventura, CA: Regal, 2003).

3. Eddie Smith, *Intercessors: How to Understand and Unleash Them for God's Glory* (Houston: SpiriTruth Publishing, 2001).

RECOMMENDED RESOURCES

Alves, Elizabeth. *Becoming a Prayer Warrior.* Ventura, CA: Regal Books, 1998.

Caballeros, Harold. *Victorious Warfare.* Nashville, TN: Thomas Nelson Books, 2001.

Cerullo, Morris. *You Can Know How to Defeat Satan.* San Diego, CA: Morris Cerullo Ministries, 2002.

Frangipane, Francis. *The Three Battlegounds.* Arrow Publications, 2006.

Greenwood, Rebecca. *Authority to Tread.* Grand Rapids, MI: Chosen Books, 2005.

Jacobs, Cindy. *Possessing the Gates of the Enemy.* Grand Rapids, MI: Chosen Books, 1991.

Murray, Andrew. *The Ministry of Intercession.* Springdale, PA: Whitaker House, 1982.

Otis, George, Jr. *Informed Intercession.* Ventura, CA: Regal Books, 1999.

—*The Last of the Giants.* Tarrytown, NY: Chosen Books, 1991.

Pierce, Chuck, and Rebecca Sytsema. *The Future War of the Church.* Ventura, CA: Regal Books, 2001.

Prince, Derek. *Shaping History Through Prayer and Fasting.* Ft. Lauderdale, FL: Derek Prince Ministries, 1973.

Sheets, Dutch. *Intercessory Prayer.* Ventura, CA: Regal Books, 1996.

—*Authority in Prayer.* Minneapolis, MN: Bethany House, 2006.

Sherrer, Quin, and Ruthanne Garlock. *The Spiritual Warrior's Prayer Guide.* Ann Arbor, MI: Servant Publications, 1992.

Sjoberg, Kjell. *Winning the Prayer War.* Chichester, England: New Wine Press, 1991.

Smith, Alice. *Beyond the Veil.* Ventura, CA: Regal Books, 1996.

—*Beyond the Lie.* Minneapolis, MN: Bethany House, 2006.

—*Delivering the Captives.* Minneapolis, MN: Bethany House, 2007.

—*Spiritual Intimacy.* Minneapolis, MN: Bethany House, 2008.

Smith, Eddie. *How to Be Heard in Heaven.* Minneapolis, MN: Bethany House, 2007.

—*Breaking the Enemy's Grip.* Minneapolis, MN: Bethany House, 2005.

Smith, Eddie, and Michael Hennen. *Strategic Prayer.* Minneapolis, MN: Bethany House, 2007.

Smith, Eddie and Alice. *Spiritual Housecleaning.* Ventura, CA: Regal Books, 2003.

—*Spiritual Housecleaning Workbook.* Ventura, CA: Regal Books, 2007.

Wagner, C. Peter. *Prayer Shield.* Ventura, CA: Regal Books, 1992.

—*Confronting the Powers.* Ventura, CA: Regal Books, 1996.

—*Praying With Power.* Ventura, CA: Regal Books, 1997.

HOW TO CONTACT EDDIE AND ALICE SMITH

Author and speaker Eddie Smith and his wife, Alice, travel worldwide, teaching on various themes related to prayer, spiritual warfare, deliverance, and discipleship.

The Smiths teach together as well as individually.

For information about hosting the Smiths or a conference in your church or city, submit your online invitation at: *www.eddieandalice.com*

PRAYER RESOURCES

Eddie and Alice Smith's books and materials, as well as other resources they recommend, can be found at: *www.prayerbookstore.com*

The Smiths also offer a FREE 52-week online school of prayer at: *www.teachmetopray.com*

FREE NEWSLETTER

Join thousands worldwide who receive *Insight*, Eddie and Alice's FREE weekly e-mail newsletter.

Subscribe at: *www.eddieandalice.com*

Eddie Smith
Eddie and Alice Smith Ministries
7710-T Cherry Park Dr., Ste. 224
Houston, TX 77095
Phone: (713) 466-4009, (800) 569-4825 (U.S. only)
Fax: (713) 466-5633
E-mail: usprayercenter@cs.com
Web site: *www.eddieandalice.com*
Resource Center: *www.prayerbookstore.com*

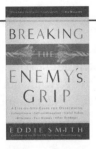

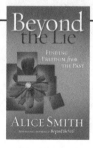